# High Finance
## on a
# Low Budget

## Other Books by Mark Skousen

*The Complete Guide to Financial Privacy*
*Dissent on Keynes*
*The Economics of a Pure Gold Standard*
*Economics on Trial*
*The Insider's Banking & Credit Almanac*
*Playing the Price Controls Game*
*Scrooge Investing*
*The Structure of Production*
*Tax Free*

# High Finance
# on a
# Low Budget

Mark Skousen

and

Jo Ann Skousen

 Dearborn
Financial Publishing, Inc.

While a great deal of care has been taken to provide accurate and current information, the ideas, suggestions, general principles and conclusions presented in this text are subject to local, state and federal laws and regulations, court cases and any revisions of same. The reader is thus urged to consult legal counsel regarding any points of law—this publication should not be used as a substitute for competent legal advice.

Publisher: Kathleen A. Welton
Associate Editor: Karen A. Christensen
Interior Design: Irving Perkins Associates
Jacket Design: One Plus One Studio

Published by Dearborn Financial Publishing, Inc.

Printed in the United States of America

93  94  95  10  9  8  7  6  5  4  3  2  1

**Library of Congress Cataloging-in-Publication Data**

Skousen, Mark.
High finance on a low budget / by Mark Skousen and Jo Ann Skousen.
—[6th rev. ed.]
p.    cm.
Includes index.
ISBN 0-79310-467-X : $19.95
1. Finance, Personal.   2. Investments.   I. Skousen, Jo Ann.
II. Title.
HG179.S528      1993
332.6'78—dc20                    92-30029
CIP

*To Mark's mother,*
Helen Louise Skousen,
*who taught him the value of work,*
*and*
*to Jo Ann's mother,*
Dorothy Mae Saunders,
*who taught her the value of money*

# Acknowledgments

HUNDREDS OF FINANCIAL ADVISERS and investment experts have contributed to this book. Among these individuals, we would like to thank Richard Band, Adrian Day, Gary Alexander, Van Simmons, Roger LeRoy Miller, Bob Kephart, Harry Browne, Doug Casey, Dave Phillips, Greg Horne, Dick Fabian, Bert Dohmen, John Pugsley, Larry Abraham, John Schaub, Bob Allen, Martin Truax, Mike Checkan, Bill Bradford, Andrew Westhem, Jim Davidson, Vern Jacobs, Bill Donoghue and John Templeton.

We also would like to thank Sheron Pitts for typing the entire manuscript, and *Harry Browne Special Reports* for permission to reprint charts for stocks, gold and silver.

Finally, we'd like to thank Kathy Welton, Bobbye Middendorf, Karen Christensen and others at Dearborn Financial Publishing for their enthusiastic support for this new edition of *High Finance on a Low Budget*.

# Contents

# Preface

IT HAS BEEN OVER ten years, five editions and a quarter of a million copies since we first wrote *High Finance on a Low Budget*. The response has been overwhelming. The subject of "no-minimum investing" continues to be popular among investors of all income levels.

Meanwhile, the financial revolution continues into the 1990s, and it's time for a new edition of this book. This sixth edition of *High Finance on a Low Budget* is completely revised, and we've added numerous new products and investment ideas. The changes are so extensive and the new additions are so large that it's almost a new book! We have greatly expanded the sections on budgeting and developing a consistent investment program. In addition, the chapters on real estate and the stock market have been greatly expanded to include the latest, most profitable techniques. Finally, all the names, addresses and telephone numbers of recommended investments, brokers and advisers have been updated.

The information herein has been carefully compiled from sources believed to be reliable, but because of changing laws and events, the information contained in this book may require updating when you receive this material.

Because no two people are alike, the advice contained in this book may not be suitable for all investors. You should send for and read carefully the prospectuses and information regarding any investment vehicle you consider.

The first rule of investing is this: *Caveat emptor*—Let the buyer beware!

Mark and Jo Ann Skousen

# High Finance
## on a
## Low Budget

# CHAPTER 1

# Welcome to the World of High Finance

*He who would catch fish, must venture his bait.*

—Poor Richard's Almanac

As FINANCIAL WRITERS AND consultants, we have received hundreds of letters each year from concerned investors. One of the most frequent letters we receive goes something like this:

> Your advice is fine for the wealthy. But what about those of us living on a limited budget—the wage earners, retirees, housewives, students and widows who have only a few thousand dollars, or less, to invest? How can we beat inflation and taxes like the rich do?

In these uncertain times of inflation, taxes and economic crises, millions of investors are coming to the painful conclusion that it takes money to make money. The small saver seems destined to a low-yielding savings account that is rapidly devoured by taxes and inflation.

The wealthy can take advantage of highly profitable venture capital deals. They can afford sophisticated money managers who profit from professional information on stocks, gold and commodities. They invest in tax shelters that sharply reduce their tax burdens and they participate in exotic foreign investments, overseas banking and money havens. But the world of high finance seems beyond the reach of small investors who don't have thousands of dollars with which to meet minimum investment requirements or insider contacts to tell them about the best deals.

In the end, it may seem that while the rich profit, millions of average, middle-class citizens must bear the brunt of costly living and inequitable taxation.

## SMALL INVESTORS CAN ESCAPE

In response to the small investor's plight, we began to research low-cost ways for the novice investor to preserve and increase capital. In preparing this material, we searched for sound investments, inflation hedges and tax-favored opportunities that would accept investments of $500 or less, and sometimes impose no minimum at all! As a result, we have discovered ways that will help anyone with a little money, a little knowledge and a little courage start down the road to high finance. We can't promise instant fortunes, but we can foresee a comfortable nest egg in just a couple of years. Little-known but effective tools are finally available to the "penny capitalist" in the lucrative fields of real estate, commodities, the stock market, precious metals and foreign investments.

In this book you will find specific information for the small investor, including names, addresses and the minimum requirements of reputable companies. In addition, you will learn how individual investment markets work, when to get out of one investment and into another and how to minimize the tax liability on your newly found wealth. Soon you will have the confidence to be your own investment adviser, and to help you get started, we have included specific portfolio recommendations in Chapter 17 to ensure a balanced mix of investments.

## HOW TO GET STARTED

You may be among the many Americans who have trouble saving $5, let alone $500. You may be reading this book not just for the "high finance" but for the "low budget" as well. If so, you'll be interested in the simple but powerful techniques we present for lowering your cost of living without lowering your standard of living, thereby allowing you to create some start-up investment capital immediately.

Successful investing and financial freedom involve two critical steps: knowledge of the investment world *and* the ability to build investment capital through saving. It is impossible to make wealth and keep it without both of these steps. Wise investors, no matter what their income, will save and invest as much as possible. Regardless of how much you make, if you fail to invest and to monitor your spending habits, you won't break away from the crowd.

Keep in mind that, when dealing in small investment amounts, commissions and fees become critical. The well-to-do investor can afford to pay substantial fees, but the small investor cannot. A $35 fee is negligible when investing $10,000, but it is a significant concern when investing $500 or less. Therefore, in our research for this book, we have tried to emphasize low commissions and fees as an essential ingredient. For example, you can buy common stocks, high-grade corporate bonds and mutual funds without a broker and without paying commissions; choose a reputable coin dealer who buys and sells gold and silver at the lowest possible premiums; or incorporate your small business for as little as $100. This book is full of specific examples.

## SUCCESS STORIES: INCREDIBLE BUT TRUE!

A decade ago, we saw an article in a newspaper that read, "Two Akron charities will each receive half of a $1 million estate from a retired General Tire Co. worker who never made more than $15,000 annually."

A young friend of ours has never made much money in his salaried job, nor has he inherited any money from relatives. But by being a careful investor, he has more than $25,000 in investment funds, which he accrued gradually through investments in stocks, bonds and gold and silver coins.

On a Caribbean cruise we met an unemployed student in his early twenties who had just made $10,000 on a real estate transaction that cost him only $2 in out-of-pocket expenses.

Recently, we listened to the story of an Atlanta woman who was married to a man making $16,000 a year. They had eight children, and she did not work outside the home, yet she said that in the previous two years she had been able to save $3,000.

Even more amazing was the Austin, Texas, man who called in during a radio talk program to tell us that he and his wife were living examples of our financial system. He said that they own an $80,000 home free and clear and drive a Mercedes-Benz—even though neither of them earns more than $15,000 a year!

How did they do it? By following the formula outlined in our book.

In the first edition of this book, published in 1981, we recommended one mutual fund that required no minimum and no broker: Twentieth Century Select Investors. If a reader had invested only $100 a month since 1981, he would have over $40,000 today. Now that's what we mean by *high finance on a low budget!*

Over the years we have received a variety of letters from individuals who have saved a remarkable amount of money on a low income. One letter came from a divorcée in Scottsmore, Florida. She wrote, "My income is approximately $8,000 a year, out of which I support my daughter and myself. . . . It seemed that I couldn't make ends meet no matter how I tried. . . . But after reading your book I made a list of all the things I could do without and was absolutely stunned at the amount I was frittering away. . . . Now, instead of having nothing I find that I can save a little each month simply by being more careful. . . ."

Another letter told the story of "Aunt Minnie." It stated, "After reading your chapter on saving, I was reminded of Aunt Minnie.

Minnie kept a daily record of her pocket money and deposited any extra cash in the bank at the end of every week. This spare change was built into a *nest egg of $20,000*, a sizeable amount in her day. It all shows what you can do with a little planning and care."

The fact is that thousands of people have built small fortunes through a simple savings and investment plan. Even more significant is the fact that these people have not lived miserly lives in the process. They have enjoyed life and have obtained many of the things that money can buy. One of the benefits of a consistent savings plan is that it gives you the freedom to spend the rest of your income in whatever way you may desire.

If these people could do it, you can, too. High finance *is* possible for the small investor making less than $20,000 a year. The steps outlined in the next few chapters will show you the way.

# CHAPTER 2

# Where Did All
# the Money Go?

*Women & wine, game & deceit,*
*make the wealth small and the wants great.*

—Poor Richard's Almanac

THE UNITED STATES IS undisputedly the wealthiest nation in the world. Americans should be living on easy street. And yet we are far from the picture of economic health.

Unemployment is high. Taxes increase yearly. Consumer debt and government spending are out of control. Respectable bankers charge interest rates that would have made a 1930s loan shark blush, while paying almost nothing to savers. In short, it seems that everything is going up except our standard of living.

In our work as financial consultants, we meet with people of all income levels, from the $20,000-a-year secretary to the millionaire entrepreneur. Most clients are seeking investment advice, but we find that an increasing number of people from all walks of life are asking the same questions: How did I get into this difficult financial situation? How can I regain control of my life?

A typical client came to us for a personal consultation. He was desperate. At the time he was earning a salary of more than

$50,000 a year, over twice the national average, yet he was in serious financial trouble. He quarreled constantly with his wife about household finances. His children were approaching college age, and he couldn't afford to pay for their education. He was in debt and couldn't save a penny. Now his company was transferring him to the West Coast, and it appeared that he would have to pay twice as much to buy a house half the size of his current home—if he could afford to buy another house at all. It seemed to him that he had nothing to show for the nearly $1 million he had earned over his lifetime. Where did it all go? And what could he do now?

This man's story was far from unusual. It's indicative of the broad nature of financial failure in this country today. In this age of high taxes and high debt, it seems that everyone is having trouble making ends meet, and it is no longer just the poor who are hurting.

## A NATION OF BIG SPENDERS

One of the biggest causes of this predicament has been the easy availability of credit, strongly encouraged by our legislators. At one time, cynical shopkeepers reworded our national motto to read, "In God we trust, all others pay cash." Now, however, the entire motto seems to be changing to "Buy now, pay later." Instant gratification is encouraged by magazine ads, TV commercials, radio jingles, even by bank tellers. Why struggle to save toward a goal when you can have the new TV or trip to the Bahamas just by signing a credit slip? After all, it's *only* $30 a month, and you don't even have to start paying for six weeks. You can afford that!

What too many consumers fail to realize until it's too late, though, is that $30 a month for the new stereo, $249 for the car, $45 for the department store, $25 for last summer's vacation, $60 for the new family-room furniture, and $35 for the videocassette recorder soon add up to more than half the family's take-home pay—and that doesn't include the house payment. As the debt builds and monthly fixed expenditures increase, less and less is left over for future necessities. Soon the family finds itself borrowing money to buy food, household items and other immediate-consumption purchases.

But Americans haven't always been mired in debt. How did we fall into this self-destructive pattern? Part of the blame lies with the example set by the federal government itself.

For years, Congress has enjoyed the free-wheeling exhilaration of deficit spending. Does a western state want money to build a dam? Give it to them! Welfare recipients need higher doles? Why not! A national foundation desires a research grant? Sure thing! But where will the money come from? Don't worry—next year's taxes will take care of that! And if they don't? Well, we can always issue more T-bills!

## ANTISAVINGS MENTALITY

This free-spending attitude on the part of our government has prevailed since the early 1960s, when Congress adopted the Keynesian philosophy of economics. According to John Maynard Keynes, an economist whose theories first gained popularity in the 1930s, the key to economic recovery is consumption. According to his theory, saving is bad because when people save their money, it is taken out of the marketplace. Fewer items are purchased, and this reduced demand causes manufacturers to cut back on production. Reduced production naturally results in worker layoffs, so unemployment rises. Those people who are now out of work are unable to purchase items, so demand is reduced even further and the economy slows down even more. According to this theory, the nation's entire economy is destroyed by savings.

Keynes's followers called this theory the "paradox of thrift," and on the surface it sounds fairly plausible. Convincing enough, at any rate, that Congress has adopted it as the basis of our national fiscal policy, and members of the news media perpetuate it as their leading economic indicator. How often do we hear news reporters urging listeners to spend their way out of the recession, especially at Christmastime? We even heard one of the morning news shows in 1991 touting the "dry-cleaning index": We must be coming out of the recession, the reporter opined, because people were taking more clothes to the dry cleaner's! The media also cheered when credit card interest rates were lowered, suggesting that easier consumer credit would be good for the economy.

But common sense cries out against such a theory. How can consumer debt, which is bad for the individual, be good for the nation as a whole? And how can saving, which is a boon to the individual, be inherently evil, as the paradox of thrift suggests? The answer, of course, is that they are not. The money that people save is not being removed from the economy in a puff of smoke; it is being saved for future consumption. While it may be true that current demand for consumer goods would be temporarily reduced by a massive, nationwide return to higher savings, that reduction would only be temporary.

Moreover, it must be remembered that all those saved funds are not being stuffed under mattresses and into coffee cans across the country. People use their savings for investments. They may invest directly by purchasing stocks or bonds, or indirectly by placing their funds in bank accounts that are then loaned by the bank to businesses, potential homeowners, car buyers and the like. Because more investment funds are available, interest rates come down, thus reducing the cost of doing business. Profits increase, and investors share in those profits through interest and dividends. When savers eventually decide to use their money to buy something, they find that their savings have multiplied, and they are now able to purchase more goods and services than would have been possible if they had spent all their money when they first received it. Demand increases, and new jobs are created.

As you can see, there is no "paradox" of thrift. Saving money may reduce current consumption temporarily, but it will stimulate business expansion in the present and greatly increase consumption in the future. When people are free from debt, with equity in their home and savings in their account, they are able to invest and spend even more freely.

## PARKINSON'S SECOND LAW IN ACTION

When individuals are asked where they think the money will come from to pay off their debts, most will look to future income for the answer. "I'm getting a raise next month" or "I can get a part-time job in the evenings" are common excuses for spending beyond one's current income. So why doesn't that extra income solve an individual's financial ills?

The experience of one family we know is a great example. When they received a small inheritance of $10,000, the wife wanted to redecorate the living room; the husband wanted to take the family on a first-class vacation; they both agreed that they needed a second car. In the end they decided to do *all three*—even though the inheritance was only enough to pay for one of the choices. Instead of enhancing their financial health, their inheritance put them deeper in debt.

This universal problem was described by Professor C. Northcote Parkinson in his classic book, *The Law and the Profits* (Houghton Mifflin, 1960). His first law, "Work expands to fill the time available," is well known and is a commentary on inefficiency and bureaucracy at work in both government and large corporations.

Parkinson's second law is less known, but is just as significant a truth: **"Expenditures rise to meet income."**

Examining the federal budget process can be extremely helpful for families and individuals who want to form a successful budgeting process of their own. Look at the way Congress plans its fiscal year, and then don't let it happen to you!

The 1982–83 fiscal budget provides a good example. President Reagan presented a budget to Congress which had an estimated deficit of $100 billion. Because of his campaign promise to balance the budget, Reagan felt uncomfortable about this huge

deficit. So he decided to reduce it somewhat by increasing revenues. Through a judicious use of television rhetoric and political
arm-twisting, he was able to push a bill through Congress that
would increase taxes by nearly $100 billion over three years. "I
don't like to do this," he claimed, "but we have to in order to
reduce the deficit." We didn't have to wait to see whether Parkinson's second law would apply, however. Before the House would
agree to the bill, it attached a rider that extended unemployment
benefits, at an extra cost of $13 billion. And, just one month later,
Congress overrode the President's veto of another spending bill,
in anticipation of the increased revenues. Result: Expenditures
immediately rose to meet income, and the deficit remained intact.

Again, in 1990 President Bush decided to push through a tax
increase—in direct violation of his "no new taxes" pledge—
ostensibly to reduce the deficit. Instead, this additional revenue
allowed a spendthrift Congress to waste even more of the taxpayers' money. Despite massive increases in tax revenues over the
decade, the deficit climbed to nearly $500 billion a year.

In many ways, individuals are like Congress. Of course, they
cannot print their own money, but they can create money through
credit card debt. They often act like Congress by spending up to
the limit of their incomes and then borrowing on top of that. As
Parkinson states, "Individual expenditure not only rises to meet
income but tends to surpass it, and probably always will."

What is needed is a program that will control expenditures and
help individuals to live within their means. In Chapter 3 we
outline a plan that will help you free yourself from Parkinson's
second law forever.

# CHAPTER 3

---

# Never Say "Budget"!

*Annual income twenty pounds,*
*Annual expenditure nineteen pounds ought six,*
*Result happiness.*
*Annual income twenty pounds,*
*Annual expenditures twenty pounds ought six,*
*Result misery.*

—CHARLES DICKENS

THE TROUBLE WITH MOST budgets is that, like diets, they are usually started too late. Like the girl who gains thirty pounds after graduation and then tries to look terrific for the ten-year reunion in just three weeks, too many families wait until they are already deeply in debt before trying to regulate their spending habits. They suddenly catch a glimpse of their flabby, sagging financial figure and decide to shape up with a strict, no-nonsense budget. But, after a month or so, these families and individuals usually become discouraged. "I tried it once, but it just didn't work!" becomes their future excuse for financial failure.

What they fail to realize is that, after years of budgetary neglect, you can't expect to achieve complete financial independence overnight. Just as there are no miracle weight-loss diets, so are there no miraculous overnight roads to riches. Successful money management takes time, motivation and persistence. But by following the advice set forth in this chapter, you can reverse the road you are traveling and make substantial progress in a matter of weeks!

Part of the problem is that budgets simply aren't fun. The very word conjures up visions of beans and macaroni three nights a week. Wearing the same frowsy coat for five years in a row. Driving ten miles across town to the cut-rate gas station. Pinching pennies till Lincoln cries, "Ouch!"

Nearly everyone has started a budget at one time or another, but very few people have kept it up. Common reasons for discarding a budget are numerous.

"It's too confining," say some.

"It's my money, and I don't want some piece of paper telling me how to spend it," say others.

"I'm already careful—I don't need a budget," boast a few.

And, "It doesn't work," observe far too many.

In fact, drawing up a formal budget is rather like embarking on a new diet. The end results are desirable, but the means of arriving at the goal often prove too difficult or too painful. A lot of the spice is taken out of life, whether you are counting calories or pennies. As a result, most people cheat a little and slip off their budgets, just as they slip off their diets.

During our research we have discovered another good reason why so many people hate to budget: **Budgets simply don't work.**

## WHY MOST BUDGETS FAIL

Over the years, people have adopted a number of budgeting techniques, with varying degrees of success.

Before the age of checking accounts and easy credit, the "envelope method" was popular. Under this system, you converted your paycheck into cash and then divided it among envelopes marked "Rent," "Food," "Utilities," "Clothing," "Lunch Money," etc. When it was time to go grocery shopping, you simply took some money from the "Food" envelope and went to the store.

One significant advantage to this system was that it was impossible to spend more than you earned. When the envelope was empty, you had to wait until the next paycheck before buying anything else.

But there are drawbacks to the envelope method. For one thing, it is very risky to have so much cash around the house. The money could get lost or stolen, even by family members. And even if you had a very secure place in which to keep the envelopes, it would be a constant source of temptation for you. Suppose your son needed a new pair of shoes, and the "Clothing" envelope was empty but the "Gas" envelope had a $20 bill in it. It would be too easy to buy the shoes with the gas money and then hope you didn't have to drive very much this month! Soon you would be borrowing so much from one envelope or another that you wouldn't know where you started, and the budget would become meaningless.

Another reason this system doesn't work anymore is the increasing convenience of checking accounts. Checks are readily accepted in most places of business, there is no risk of losing cash, and it's always with you—you don't have to run home and get some money from the envelope when you need to make a purchase. Moreover, credit cards are even easier to use than checks. In the example cited above, it would be very tempting simply to purchase the shoes with a credit card and then worry about replenishing the "Clothing" envelope next month. It wouldn't take long for this "temporary" borrowing to get out of hand and, again, the budget would become useless.

In recent years a more sophisticated variation of the envelope method has been developed and is used by the majority of those who keep a regular budget. This method uses a list of regular expenditures, similar to the categories that would have been written on envelopes in the first method. An amount is assigned to each category, and a running total is kept of expenditures to make sure they don't exceed the allotted amount. It takes a little self-discipline at first to remember to record all expenses, but once that becomes a habit, it is an easy, straightforward method.

Most financial counselors use this method to help people gain control of their spending.

So why doesn't it work for most people? A Gallup poll reported that four out of ten Americans claim to keep a budget, yet over two-thirds of them admit that they do not stay within its allotments. Why the high rate of failure?

Chief on the list of reasons is that the budget is too confining. Americans simply don't like having to check with the book each time they want to buy something. They consider themselves to be careful enough with their money already. After all, no one is intentionally wasteful! Moreover, they don't like the subservient role of having to ask permission, even though they are checking with a budget they drew up themselves.

Another reason for budget-book failure is that expenditure goals are often unrealistic. It is not unusual for a family to sit down together and write up a budget without first having any idea of how much they have already been spending for various things. For years they may have been vaguely aware of the costs of specific items, without ever realizing what their total expenditures have been. In short, they have no idea where all their money has been going, so in developing a budget, they set down arbitrary amounts that sound reasonable, making sure that the grand total does not exceed monthly income. Then they snap the book shut with a satisfied sigh. "That should be the end of our financial troubles!" they conclude with a smile.

But what happens at the end of the month? There is often a lot of finger-pointing and excuse-making as each family member tries to explain about the unexpected expenses that came up "just this once." Adjustments may be made and the budget tried again, but too often this marks the end of budgeting for yet another family.

## NO IDEAL BUDGET

Other families or individuals, recognizing the fact that they have no idea how much should be allotted for each category, may turn to the experts for help. The U.S. Bureau of Labor Statistics, as well as private household financial counselors, publish guidelines that show what the average American spends on various major items. For example, a recent study found that the average family of four spends approximately $150 per week for food. Most studies agree that 25 to 30 percent of take-home pay is usually spent for housing, 10 percent for transportation, 7 percent for clothing, and so forth. Comparing your own expenditures with these national averages can be very interesting, but they aren't really very helpful in determining what you "should" be spending.

The problem with this approach is that no two people and no two families are exactly alike. You may have a health problem that requires you to spend more than the national average for medical expenses, while the fact that you have a garden and eat only home-canned fruits and vegetables may greatly reduce the amount of money you spend on food. Similarly, if you can take advantage of a good public transit system you may spend less than the average 10 percent for transportation. On the other hand, your children's expensive piano lessons don't appear anywhere on the "ideal" budget—does that mean they should be eliminated?

This brings us to the major drawback of formal budget systems, and the reason we have titled this chapter, "Never Say 'Budget'!" In our work as financial consultants, we have found that a strict allocation-type budget is actually self-defeating. It is almost impossible to spend exactly what the budget allocates. Consequently, if you go over your budget, you will feel like a failure, become discouraged and eventually give up.

Even worse, if you *underspend* your allotment, you may end up spending more, simply because "the book allows it." Instead of just keeping up with the Joneses, you are now keeping up with the national average! Either way, the budget book becomes a taunting taskmaster, and you will learn to resent it.

## AN EASY WAY TO CONTROL RUNAWAY SPENDING

Despite the difficulty of developing a budget, we do not recommend that you simply continue spending indiscriminately. There is a right way to control your spending habits, and it begins to work immediately.

We recently asked a self-made millionaire the secret of his success. He and his wife had married during the Depression and started out with nothing. He had a job, but at the end of each month they found that all their money was gone, and they really had nothing to show for it. They were determined to do more than just break even all their lives, however, so they decided to evaluate their expenditures. *They began writing down everything they spent, even the smallest items.* Soon they had a clear picture of where their money was going. Next they established a regular savings program, which they called their "stake." This was their investment capital, which they would use eventually to start a business of their own. They continued to keep an accurate record of their expenditures and evaluated it regularly. "We just didn't make impulsive purchases," they said, "because we knew it would take money away from our stake." These people are far from miserly. They raised and educated five children, have set up separate trust funds to which they contribute regularly for each of their grandchildren and have always made generous charitable contributions. They enjoy life. But they have learned the secret of how to avoid wasting money and have become extremely wealthy.

We have found that when people examine their own spending habits, two things generally happen. First, they are often shocked to discover where their money has been going. "We can't be eating that much!" is a common reaction. Second, and more significantly, they automatically begin to make adjustments that will cut the waste from their monthly expenditures, without having to establish a formal budget.

In a personal economics course we teach at Rollins College, we require students to keep track of their daily expenses during the semester. At the end of the course, the vast majority are shocked by how much they "wasted" on going to restaurants for lunch and dinner. Many decide to cut down by bringing their own lunch to work or by making dinner at home. It's a valuable exercise.

Once you have decided to use this "no budget" budget, you

will find that it is very easy to implement. Simply get a small notebook and start writing down everything you buy. It helps to list your expenditures in specific categories, so you can see your running total at a glance for evaluating purposes. You can use a simple spiral notebook, or you may prefer to purchase a ready-made list such as Hallmark's "Household Budget and Expenses." It allows you to keep track on a daily, weekly, monthly and yearly basis.

*Write down everything you spend, every day.* At first it may seem difficult to remember, but don't give up. Psychologists have learned that it takes just three weeks to make or break a habit. If you keep a conscientious record for 21 days, it will become an automatic action that will help you control your spending for life.

Many people are shocked when they discover how much they spend every month or year on cigarettes, magazines, cosmetics, snacks, impulse items and entertainment. In some cases the cost is considered worthwhile. Other times it's an extravagance. Some smokers, for example, will continue to buy the same amount of cigarettes no matter what they cost. Others will cut down after seeing how much it's costing them. One family we counseled subscribed to every newsmagazine, several specialty magazines, and both the morning and afternoon newspapers. They had so much reading material coming into their home that they often threw out one issue completely unread when the next issue arrived. By deciding to eliminate some of their subscriptions, this family reduced its annual expenditures by several hundred dollars.

## Added Bonus: Marital Harmony

Most families who use this method of money management discover an added bonus—besides gaining control of their finances, they also improve the quality of their family life. Marriage counselors agree that money is one of the principal causes of marital discord. One accuses, the other excuses, but no one really knows who is to blame. By finally and completely answering the question, "Where did all the money go?" this system can eliminate the major source of financial fights. As one husband said, "I had no idea there were so many little expenses involved in maintaining a family. My wife has been doing a great job with her household allowance, but I just didn't realize it before!"

Having a specific savings goal also adds to marital harmony. Like our millionaire friends who were saving for their "stake," couples who share a long-range investment goal no longer play financial blackmail, a disastrous game in which one person decides, "If you're going to spend money on something foolish that you want, I'm going to spend at least as much money on something I want!"

Writing everything down may not be the answer for everybody, however. Some people just never get into the habit of listing all their expenditures, down to the chewing gum they buy at the drugstore. One man who liked to stop off for a few beers with his buddies on the way home from work Friday nights was amazed to find that those "few beers" were costing almost as much as his wife spent on groceries for an entire week! Instead of changing his habits, however, he said, "We are not keeping records anymore. . . . I don't want anyone telling me I'm spending too much on beer and stock-car races!" He will continue to hide the truth from his family and from himself, and his wife will continue trying to get by on what's left over.

But for those who are serious about wanting to gain control of their spending habits, recording and evaluating past expenditures is an important beginning. It allows you to make intelligent choices about what you will and will not buy, and it eventually gives you the freedom to spend without worry.

If this process seems to be time-consuming, be assured that you will not need to do this for the rest of your life. We have found that a year of intensive self-evaluation is generally enough time for most people to change their attitudes about money and gain control of their spending habits. You may want to resume the written system occasionally when you face major financial changes—growing family, changing income levels, moving to a new town or adjusting to inflation, for example—but, after that, the evaluation techniques will become an automatic, subconscious element of your spending decisions.

## A BETTER ALTERNATIVE TO BUDGETING

We conclude that strict formal budgeting will never work for most Americans for one overwhelming reason: It requires a lot of hard work and discipline over a long period of time. Too many forces are at work making it easy to go off the budget—easy credit, impulse buying, inflation and government tax policies that encourage spending. Writing it all down, item by item, on a daily basis will help you get hold of your financial picture.

As dieters know, there is more than one way to lose weight. You can eat less without altering your lifestyle, or you can exercise more. Exercise may seem harder at first, but it can result in a healthier, more vital physique, one that can say good-bye to restrictive, calorie-counting diets forever.

So it is with your financial health. There is more than one road to financial security, and this chapter has shown you the most successful way. If you study it carefully and apply the principles diligently, you may never say "budget" again.

# CHAPTER 4

# Cut Your Cost of Living Without Cutting Your Standard of Living

*Economy is in itself a source of great revenue.*

—SENECA

IF YOU HAVE BEEN spending all the money you earn up until now (and perhaps even a little more than you earn through credit cards), you might be thinking, "But I can't cut back anywhere. I don't waste any money, and I need every penny I earn just to cover day-to-day expenses!" While it may be true that no one intentionally wastes money, it is equally true that everyone spends more than they need to on certain items. The tips in this chapter may help you find places in your own budget where you can reduce your cost of living painlessly. These areas include:

- Housing
- Insurance
- Taxes
- Transportation

- Food

- Clothing

- Bargain shopping

According to an extensive survey conducted by the U.S. Bureau of Labor Statistics, Americans live on a wide variety of budgets. Imagine the savings that would result if a high-income family could adjust itself to a middle-income family's habits!

## HOUSING: SHOULD YOU RENT OR BUY?

Housing takes one of the biggest chunks out of your monthly budget—from 25 to 35 percent for the average family. If you could reduce your housing costs and invest the money you saved, you would be well on your way to financial security.

Home ownership is still the American dream, but that dream became a nightmare for many in the 1980s and 1990s, when falling prices, tighter mortgage markets and rising closing costs made it more difficult to buy and sell real estate, especially for those on low budgets. Is it always better to buy than rent?

Monthly mortgage payments are much higher than rent for a comparable house, even if you make a substantial down payment. You lose liquidity with your investment funds as well as flexibility (the freedom to move unexpectedly, for example) because houses often take several weeks or months to sell. In addition, maintenance costs can be expensive and unexpected, destroying a budget that is already tight.

We discuss real estate as an investment in Chapter 9, but in this section we address housing as a cost of living that can be reduced temporarily as you search for ways to increase your savings base.

There are times when renting makes sense, even though it builds no equity. Selling a home can cost as much as 10 percent in commissions, legal fees and other charges, and if it takes several months to sell, you will have to continue making monthly payments. In times of rapidly rising inflation, your increased selling price can compensate for these costs, but in slower markets it may be wiser to rent temporarily while building equity in your savings account, particularly if you expect to move again in less than two years.

Making temporary sacrifices in housing can lead to long-term satisfaction. For example, when we were first married, we considered renting a townhouse in a trendy development where some of our friends lived, but the rent was high and we would have had to borrow money for furniture as well. Half our income would have been spent on housing! Instead, we rented a furnished basement apartment for one-third the cost and put the difference into the bank. Within three years we were able to buy a lovely four-bedroom house. Three years of cutting back led to a lifetime of comfortable homes and real estate equity.

There are other ways to reduce the cost of housing. If you rent an apartment or duplex, you could offer to perform repairs, maintenance and other management tasks in exchange for a reduced rent. If you don't require the permanence of a long-term lease, you could look around for a house that is empty and for sale. Tell the owners you will keep it in showable condition and be willing to move when it sells if they will give you a good rental rate. The advantages to the owner are that a house looks better to potential buyers when it is furnished, the property is protected from vandals when it isn't empty, and the rental income is money they would not otherwise receive.

Save the difference to use for the down payment when you finally are ready to buy. Read our chapter on real estate for suggestions on smart ways to reduce your mortgage costs and purchasing price.

## How To Reduce the Cost of Borrowing

If you decide to buy a home, you should be aware that your interest payments over the course of the loan will often total two to three times the amount you actually borrow. For example, if you borrow $100,000 at 11 percent for 30 years, your interest payments alone will total a whopping $242,846.78!

One easy way to drastically reduce your interest payments and build equity faster is to prepay additional principal. For example, if you paid just $36.64 extra the second month of the loan just described, you would eliminate $914.35 from the total interest cost—comparable to a return of nearly 2,500 percent! Multiply those extra payments, and you will multiply the savings. The more you pay, the more you save. By making one extra payment each year, you can reduce the life of your mortgage by as much as one-third! Some mortgage companies impose prepayment penalties, however, so check with your finance company first.

## INSURANCE: CUT COSTS BY MORE THAN 50 PERCENT

One of the items for which you spend a great deal of money without receiving any particular pleasure is insurance. It is an important expenditure, something everyone should have, but there is no sense of status or enjoyment received from it. It's not an area for keeping up with the Joneses. In fact, if you could receive adequate coverage for less money, the Joneses wouldn't even know, let alone care.

Surprisingly, you may need less life insurance than you think. If you are unmarried with no dependents, or if your children are on their own, you really don't need anything beyond burial costs. If you fit this category, put your premium payments to better use by investing in something with a higher return.

Most people, though, do need life insurance to support dependent family members, to pay funeral expenses and to provide liquidity so assets will not have to be sold to pay estate taxes or to satisfy debts. Buying the right insurance product and getting the best deal on your insurance can save hundreds or thousands of dollars over your lifetime.

A major revolution is occurring in the insurance industry that can mean substantial reductions in premiums and wiser investments if you switch to a new life insurance policy. You may have bought the best term policy available three years ago, but there could easily be another company today that offers a better program for a better price.

Some of the innovations that have taken place concern whole-life policies and single-premium annuities, products that combine life insurance with excellent investment possibilities and favorable tax treatment. Talk to an independent insurance agent, one who deals with many companies and thus can find the best policy for you, about these and other insurance products. David T. Phillips is an independent insurance brokerage firm with nationwide coverage with whom we've dealt for a long time. You can contact Phillips at 3200 N. Dobson Rd., Bldg. C, Chandler, AZ 85224, 800-223-9610 or 602-897-6088.

The rates for other forms of insurance, such as medical, auto, homeowners and casualty, have risen abominably in recent years. We strongly recommend a high deductible to reduce the cost of premiums. You should think of your insurance policy as disaster coverage, not as prepaid expenditures. Insurance companies are quick to cancel policies or raise premiums when numerous claims are filed. For example, accidents and traffic tickets remain on your record for three years, and your rates are adjusted accordingly. You are better off paying a $700 fender-bender repair yourself and avoiding a rate increase of 10 to 20 percent that will be in effect for the next three years.

Another way to reduce your cost of auto insurance is to buy it from the same company that carries your homeowners insurance. You may get a discount of up to 20 percent. Again, with homeowners insurance, avoid making small claims that could lead to cancellation. We have a neighbor who had a continuing problem with lightning causing electrical damage to her home's security system and the pipes. Each repair was minor—about $500. But after three such claims she was told, "One more claim and your policy will be canceled." It may not seem fair, but it is a fact of life that insurance companies don't grease the squeaky wheel—they cancel it.

Medical insurance, even with group plans, is almost prohibitively expensive these days unless it is a fringe benefit of the company where you work. If you must insure yourself, we strongly recommend a high deductible. A deductible of $500 or $1,000 is not unreasonable. The higher your salary, the higher the deductible should be. You need insurance against catastrophic illnesses and injuries, but in most cases your routine office visits will cost less than the insurance premiums. A high deductible can reduce your premiums by an average of 30 percent annually. Check with several insurance companies, and ask what the premiums would be, based on various deductibles.

Self-employed individuals often pay extremely high premiums for health insurance because they cannot take advantage of employer group rates. However, you might be able to get group coverage through a fraternal, professional or civic organization. Contact the alumni association of the school from which you graduated, a professional or business organization for which you qualify or hobby clubs. We once obtained Blue Cross/Blue Shield coverage by joining the Texas Cattlefeeders Association when we made an investment in cattle.

Another option that is becoming increasingly popular across the country is to join a health maintenance organization (HMO). The HMO generally costs more than standard insurance, but its coverage includes routine office visits and checkups, with no deductible. The advantage is that you know exactly what your medical costs will be each month, whether you use your coverage or not. The disadvantage is that you are limited to the physicians and facilities provided by the HMO. Often, however, these include some of the best physicians in the area.

Finally, to reduce your insurance expenditures, never buy specialty insurance. Collision damage on rental cars, air-travel insurance, mortgage credit life insurance, credit card disability insurance and other specific policies are always high-priced and often unnecessary. Moreover, by using a major credit card you can often receive coverage for free.

## OVERPAYING YOUR TAXES

Overpayment of income taxes is one of the most glaring examples of needless waste. The withholding of taxes by your employer makes it easy for you to ignore how much money you send to Washington every year. The fact that most people receive a refund gives them a false feeling that Uncle Sam will make sure they don't overpay, but Uncle Sam has only the taxpayer's own figures to go by in determining how much the government will keep. In far too many cases, overpaid taxes become money that you will never see again, and money that will probably be mismanaged by the government. There is nothing patriotic about overpaying your taxes.

The amount by which people are overpaying their taxes is astonishing. An estimated one-third of American families overpay because of ignorance of the tax law. This is not because taxpayers are unintelligent, but because Congress and the IRS have made regulations so complicated that even many lawyers have trouble determining exactly what is owed.

Another reason many people overpay their taxes is that they are afraid. The IRS has done such a good job of creating fear through its "partners" in the national press and news media that many people would rather overpay than risk going through the harrowing experience of an audit. This is exactly what the IRS wants. They have only enough agents to audit 2 percent of the tax returns filed annually, so they must rely on "voluntary compliance" from the other 98 percent. Consequently, they want to intimidate citizens to the point that, when they are faced with a gray area of tax deduction, they will choose to pay it rather than claim it.

An audit is not a pleasant experience by any means, but it does not have to be as bad as most people would expect. If you keep accurate records to back up your deductions, use a tax specialist to represent you, and confine yourself to answering questions as briefly and specifically as possible, you can get through the ordeal without too much agony. An audit is rather like a trip to the dentist. You wouldn't pull all your teeth just to avoid cavities, and you shouldn't overpay your taxes just to avoid an audit, either.

It would be impossible for us to say where you specifically are overpaying your taxes. Frequently, tax deductions are overlooked simply because you fail to take the time to review all your expenses during the year, or because your records are so haphazard that you forget certain deductible expenditures. Our "no budget" method of writing down everything you spend will help you overcome this problem.

On the other hand, you may be unaware that certain expenses are deductible, whether they be medical expenses, casualty losses, interest charges or state and local taxes. Often your tax preparer is the guilty party because he or she does not take the time to ask in-depth questions about last year's expenditures or to make you aware of changes in the tax law. A handy list of possible tax deductions can be found in a free IRS publication called "Your Individual Income Tax."

Lack of tax planning early in the year can be more serious than overlooked tax deductions. It is amazing how many frantic phone calls tax-shelter brokers receive in late December from clients who suddenly realize that they earned "too much" money and will be socked with exorbitant tax bills in April. You can reduce your taxes substantially by engaging in a little tax planning. Once you have reduced your taxes legally, you can increase your exemptions on your W4 form and put that extra money to work in a long-term savings plan.

## TRANSPORTATION: CUT COSTS 30 TO 40 PERCENT

Most people buy a new car every two or three years. Other than a home, it represents the largest individual purchase made by most families. It makes sense, therefore, that if you can reduce your transportation costs, you can greatly reduce your overall expenditures.

The biggest savings in transportation can be achieved by purchasing a used car. More than half of all Americans in the market for an automobile generally buy a new car, either as a form of status gratification or to avoid buying someone else's troubles. They want a warranty to cover repair costs. But you can save thousands of dollars by buying a used car instead of a new one, which can more than offset any repair bills. Moreover, most bugs are worked out in the first year of car ownership, so by buying used you can avoid those time-consuming, albeit warranty-covered, trips to the repair shop.

Hertz Rent-A-Car Corp. conducted a study that demonstrates the incredible savings available if you purchase a used car that is two or three years old. The following chart compares the savings over a new car model, based on the age of the used car. The study took into account both the price of the car and the average operating expense over three years.

| Age of Used Car at Purchase | Percent Savings over New Car Costs Kept for 3 Years |
|---|---|
| 1 Year | 10% |
| 2 Years | 30% |
| 3 Years | 48% |
| 4 Years | 51% |
| 5 Years | 52% |
| 6 Years | 53% |
| 7 Years | 53% |

As the chart demonstrates, the greatest percentage of savings is realized on the purchase of a car two to three years old. After several years, it makes little difference whether you buy a four-year-old or seven-year-old car.

Our own experience suggests that you can achieve even greater savings than the Hertz figures show. Recently we purchased two used cars that were each only a year old and in very good condition. Together we saved about $6,000 over the price we would have had to pay if we had purchased the cars new. Thus, a late-model used car can offer you all the comforts and "newness" of a new car while saving you thousands of dollars.

The classified section of the newspaper is the best place to shop for a used car, rather than the local used-car dealer. When you buy a car through the classifieds, you are able to meet the owner, determine driving habits and ask about the car's past performance. A car dealer, on the other hand, may know little or nothing about the previous owners of the cars on the lot. Before you buy, always have an experienced mechanic check out the used car for you. Also, review the repair records of the car, and check to see if the car has been in an accident.

If you are unable to find the car you want through the classifieds and decide to purchase through a dealer, go to the dealer who specializes in the model you want. If you want to buy a Ford, go to a Ford dealer. Remember, these used cars have been used as trade-ins in most cases. Don't buy the Honda that made the previous owner trade it for a Chevy!

When you buy a new car from a dealer, be wary of terminology. Dealers can offer to sell "at cost," for example, because they receive a "selling bonus" from the manufacturer after the sale. Consequently, their official invoice actually reflects a retail price, and you should not use it as your base for negotiating. For a computer printout of a dealer's actual cost for a basic model and its option package, contact *Consumer Reports Auto Price Service* (Box 8005, Novi, MI 48050) or *Nationwide Auto Brokers* (800-521-7257). There is a nominal fee of about $10 for each printout—well worth the cost. If you are buying or selling a used car, read back copies of *Consumer Reports'* annual auto issue, *The NADA Used Car Guide,* or the *Kelley Blue Book* at your local library. You can also get an idea of a car's value by asking a bank how much they would value it for loan purposes.

## FOOD: CUT COSTS 20 TO 30 PERCENT

Overspending for food is one of the most common ways that Americans waste money and should be one of the easiest places to cut down. Food is a family's most flexible expense but also can be the most controversial. "We are what we eat," the saying goes, and sometimes we can be very emotional about food.

A number of studies reveal the shocking waste in food purchases. For example, a University of Arizona study showed that the average family *throws out* 15 percent of the food on the table! Another study, conducted by the Michigan Agriculture Experiment Station, confirmed the fact that most people shop first, then make up the menu. Consequently, the majority of people usually buy twice as many items as they planned. According to the Berkeley Consumers Cooperative, when several women started keeping track of their spending, they found that they were making *60 unplanned* purchases a month!

Few people shop around for the best food bargains. The average shopper spends only 20 minutes on each shopping trip. A Stanford University study demonstrated that shopping for specials can reduce food costs by an average of 10 percent. A similar study by the University of Arizona showed that shopping sales saved 20 percent on food items.

But remember also that time is money. One consumer counselor we know admits to spending countless hours and untold gallons of gas driving from one store to another. Once she drove 30 miles to buy chickens that were on sale for 49 cents a pound. The following week her corner grocer was selling chickens for nearly the same price. Bargain hunting is a hobby for her, but for most people shopping is something to be done as quickly and efficiently as possible.

Here are some simple rules to help cut your food bill by 10 percent or more *without* affecting the quality of your meals:

- Plan menus before shopping, and take a list with you.

- Shop bargain sales, and plan meals around seasonal specials.

- Buy in bulk when possible, but make sure you will be able to use the larger amount without throwing it out.

- Shop less frequently to reduce the temptation for impulse purchases. One study shows that by grocery shopping once every two weeks, most people's grocery bills fell by 10 to 20 percent.

Sometimes, lower-cost food items can benefit your diet and your pocketbook at the same time. We were spending as much as one-third of our grocery bill on beverages, especially in the summer. Then we purchased a water purifier, and we now serve fresh, sparkling ice water with our meals rather than soft drinks or juice. Even our children enjoy drinking water during the day when it tastes good.

## CLOTHING

Next to food, clothing is probably the biggest category where wasteful spending occurs, and one of the easiest categories on which to cut back. Evaluate your expenditures list and see where your downfalls lie. If you are an impulse shopper, get in the habit of asking the clerk to hold the item for you for 24 hours. Often this cooling-off period will help you overcome the impulse. Also, never bring two items home with the intention of taking one back after you decide which you like best. It is too easy to keep them both.

Plan ahead to avoid high-priced necessities. If you know a special event is coming, shop well in advance so you don't panic under time constraints and end up spending more than you should, just to get to the airport or party on time. This is good advice for the purchase of gifts and other nonroutine items as well. How often have you purchased a wedding, birthday or graduation gift on the way to the event, selecting something you don't particularly like at a price much higher than you were planning to spend? Planning ahead can give you greater satisfaction at a lower price for all your purchases.

Shop sales at your favorite designer store. Our children love the style at The Gap, for example, and we appreciate the quality. Best of all, their clothing moves from the new-arrivals rack to the sale rack in just four to six weeks. Our children have learned that a little patience can get them two to three times as much clothing for their money.

Look for quality and timelessness. A bargain that frays after one washing or that becomes outdated after one season is not really a bargain. Coordinate your colors and styles for versatility.

## BARGAIN SHOPPING

The classifieds can be a great place for bargain hunting for products and items that are essentially new but are offered at drastically reduced prices. Spend the next couple of days browsing through the classified section of your newspaper, and you'll be amazed at the bargains. Other sources for purchasing secondhand items include auctions, flea markets, garage sales and secondhand stores.

Secondhand stores are becoming very popular, even among the wealthy. You can find these stores listed in the Yellow Pages under specific categories, such as furniture, clothing, musical instruments, etc. Secondhand stores either purchase or take consignments of used goods, reselling them at a modest markup. You get a wider selection than can generally be found at a garage sale or in the classifieds, and you also have a legitimate, ongoing business to turn to in case something is seriously wrong with your purchase.

Pawnshops are also becoming a respectable place to purchase good-quality jewelry, electronic equipment, sports gear and other expensive items. Once relegated to seedier neighborhoods as a source of ready cash for the down-and-out, pawnshops are now moving into middle-class neighborhoods to serve as a broker between sellers and buyers as well as provide collateralized short-term loans. We don't recommend using pawnshops for loans because the interest rate and fees are so high, but they are good places to hunt for bargains.

What about the danger of inadvertently buying stolen property? Pawnbrokers are required to report all items they take in each day to the sheriff's department. Anything reported stolen will be returned to the proper owners. Moreover, items are held a minimum of 30 days before being made available for sale. These safeguards help assure that you are buying used, but not stolen, goods.

## Beware of Consumer Catchwords

Whenever you are looking for bargains, you should be aware of consumer catchwords that could result in excessive or wasteful spending. The word *savings* itself can be particularly deceptive. "On Sale! Save 50 percent or more!" the ads claim. Recently we saw a television commercial in which the husband exclaims, "I don't ask my wife how much she spent; I ask her how much she saved!" when she shops at a particular bedding store. Needless to say, that kind of attitude leads quickly to the poorhouse. Spending less is *not* necessarily the same as saving money. No one ever saved money by going on a shopping spree, even if all the purchases were "bargains." In fact, a bargain has jokingly been defined as "something you don't need at a price you can't afford to pass up."

You don't save money by spending money. Finding a bargain is meaningful only if it's something you were planning to purchase in the first place. But if you are the type of person who can't pass up an item because it's so cheap, you are probably already in serious financial trouble.

Another term whose misuse is gaining popularity is the word *investment.* Today, a car is called an "investment," a new suit is an "investment" and a quart of oil is an "investment." This is complete nonsense, of course, an illusion created by the effects of inflation. A true investment is something that increases in value, not something that you can use up or wear out. Most used consumer items sell at prices far below their original value—especially furniture and appliances. Just look at the numerous "investments" that have ended up in garage sales and secondhand stores for evidence of this fact.

## HOW TO GENERATE CASH

Don't ignore the possibility of selling what you don't need. If you are like most American families, you have dozens of unused articles and appliances lying around that you could sell for some extra cash. Take an inventory of your possessions, and get rid of the things you don't use or need. Sell big ticket items, like an old TV, radio, lawnmower, refrigerator or bed, through the classified ads. Other items, such as toys, books, clothing and kitchen supplies, can be sold at a yard sale.

But don't be like a college classmate of ours. Periodically this woman would feel guilty about having spent so much money on clothing and would sell her top-quality clothes for a fraction of what she paid for them, just to ease her conscience. Then a week or two later she would look in her closet, see that she really did have "nothing to wear" and go on a shopping spree with her credit card. Her sales were a real boon to those who bought her nearly new clothes, but they were a foolish attempt on her part to cover up her extravagance.

Incidentally, many people mistakenly believe that cash received from selling used items is taxable. The IRS would like you to think so. But in fact this money is not taxable because you are selling the items for less than you paid for them. Of course, if your used item turns out to have been a real investment and you sell it for more than the original purchase price, it would then be subject to capital gains taxes, and you would owe tax on the difference between your purchasing and selling price.

## CUT THE COST OF BANKING

You can save money by shopping around for the best checking account—often without leaving your own bank. Most banks offer a variety of account options, from the basic service-charge-plus-per-check-fee to interest-bearing accounts that charge no monthly fees at all. So-called "VIP" accounts are often available for customers who have an auto loan or home mortgage through the bank, as well as for those who have paychecks automatically deposited. Look around. If you write more than 25 checks per month, as we do, free checking can save $50 to $100 each year.

Save money on your checks as well. Most people order their checks through the bank, but you can save 50 percent on check-printing charges by ordering your checks through a private company such as Current. Contact:

Current, Inc.
1025 E. Woodman Rd.
Colorado Springs, CO 80918
800-426-0822

## YOU CAN GET MORE FOR LESS

These are just a few of the major areas where most people can easily reduce their expenditures. As you evaluate your own situation, you may find that you can cut down on entertainment, long-distance calls, eating out, clothing, etc., without really missing them. In some cases, self-evaluation may actually *increase* your standard of living. A woman we know always bought the cheapest shoes she could find, generally at a variety store rather than at a shoe store. She never thought she was wasting money because she was buying the cheapest shoes available. But after using our system of recording all her expenditures, she was amazed to discover how many pairs of shoes she bought each year. Either a strap would break or the heels would wear out, and since they weren't worth repairing, she would replace them with another cheap pair. Once she realized how much she was spending on shoes each year, she decided to buy good-quality leather shoes that could last two or three years instead of two or three months. They fitted better, looked better, lasted longer and in the long run cost less.

Many Americans believe the false notion that you need more income to live better lives and have a higher standard of living. Workers will go on strike demanding a 15-cent raise, and then spend that money foolishly without a second thought. As we have shown in this chapter, though, you can get the same quality, or even better quality, by being a careful shopper and becoming aware of your spending patterns. You can significantly reduce your cost of living without reducing your standard of living. Even though you are spending less, you will sense a greater feeling of financial freedom than you have ever felt before.

Most people constantly worry, hoping they might have something left over at the end of the month to save for the future. In the next chapter we teach you the second step to financial independence. By putting savings first, you will have the confidence of knowing that your future is secure, and consequently you will have the freedom to enjoy spending the rest of your hard-earned money.

# CHAPTER 5

# The 10 Percent Solution

*A part of all you earn is yours to keep.*

—GEORGE CLASON,
The Richest Man in Babylon

In old Babylon there once lived a certain very rich man named Arkad. Far and wide he was famed for his wealth. Also was he famed for his liberality. He was generous in his charities. He was generous with his family. He was liberal in his own expenses. But nevertheless each year his wealth increased more rapidly than he spent it.

Thus does George Clason describe the title character in his classic book, *The Richest Man in Babylon*. What was Arkad's secret? Did he inherit great wealth from his family? Was he a cunning businessman? Did he deal in illegal activities? Arkad's friends wondered, too. Clason's book continues:

And there were certain friends of younger days who came to him and said: "You, Arkad, are more fortunate than we. You have become the richest man in all Babylon while we struggle for existence. You can wear the finest garments and you can enjoy the rarest foods, while we must be content if we can clothe our families in raiment that is presentable and feed them as best we can.

"Yet, once we were equal. We studied under the same master. We played in the same games. And in neither the studies nor the games did you outshine us. And in the years since, you have been no more honorable a citizen than we.

"Nor have you worked harder or more faithfully, insofar as we can judge. Why, then, should a fickle fate single you out to enjoy all the good things of life and ignore us who are equally deserving?"

Arkad gladly shared with them his wisdom. He said that he had found the road to riches when he realized this simple truth: "A part of all you earn is yours to keep." His friends laughed at first, thinking that all they earned was theirs to keep, not just a part. But then they realized that all their money went to someone else: to the baker, the sandal maker, the tax collector, the wine seller and so forth. Nothing was left over, nothing was theirs to keep. But Arkad was different. Early on, he had decided that he would be more than a laborer all his life, and that would require having a "stake." He began to set aside one-tenth of all his earnings. At first it was hard, but it soon became a habit and he no longer even missed the money that he saved. He learned through experience how to invest wisely, and his savings multiplied until he became a wealthy man. Remember, too, that Arkad was far from miserly. He was generous with his family, his friends and himself. As long as he set aside his savings first, he felt free to spend the remaining portion in any way he liked.

You can apply this simple principle to your own life. Your savings will grow rapidly if you pay yourself first. *Reward yourself immediately by putting savings ahead of all else*—before your bills, before clothing, before the rent and even before food on the table. This may seem like a drastic measure, particularly if you have a lot of debt, but it will reap enormous dividends over the years. *Putting savings first is a critical first step. If you don't follow it, you will never have "enough."*

## HOW MUCH IS ENOUGH?

How much should you save? Presumably, the more income you earn, the easier it should be to save. Some people save 10 percent, while others save as much as half their income. But Americans are notoriously poor savers. As a nation, we save only 5.3 percent of our disposable incomes today. When based on gross income, the percentage is even more dismal. An appalling number of Americans have no savings at all outside of company retirement plans!

The fact is that foreigners are much more oriented toward savings than are Americans. Figure 5.1 compares the rate of savings in the United States with that of other major countries.

**Figure 5.1**

National Savings Rates (Average, 1960–89)

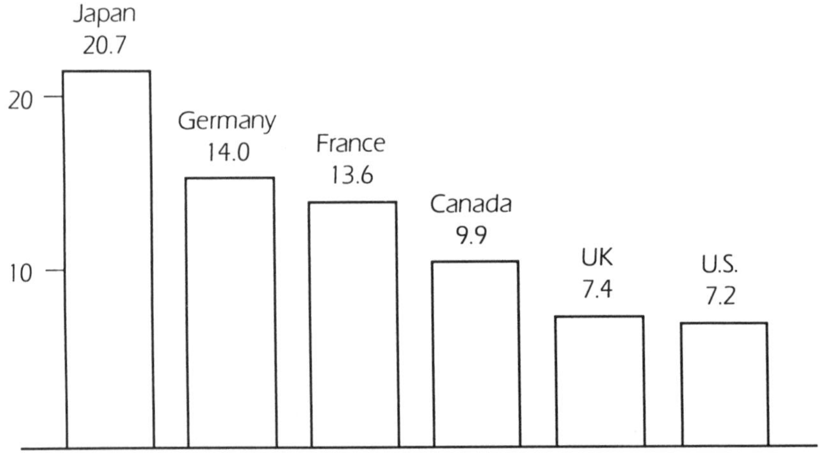

Source: U.S. Department of Commerce

## ANTISAVINGS MENTALITY IN THE UNITED STATES

Over the years there has been a decline in the U.S. savings rate. Figure 5.2 illustrates the problem.

There are many reasons the U.S. savings rate is so low. Chief among these is that U.S. government policy has discouraged savings and encouraged wasteful consumption for many years. Tax rates have been extremely high on interest earned from savings accounts, with no exemption. As a *Fortune* magazine article on the subject concluded, "The U.S. is the only major nation that provides no broad-based relief on interest income." Until recently, interest paid on most loans was deductible, giving Americans an incentive to borrow money and remain in debt. Even today, through liberal home equity loans, consumer debt can still be made tax deductible.

Fortunately, the average investor has found new alternatives to passbook accounts, such as money market funds and global income funds. The improved rates of return on money funds and other short-term debt instruments have enhanced the desirability of savings in the 1980s. But lower interest rates in the early 1990s drove the savings rate even lower.

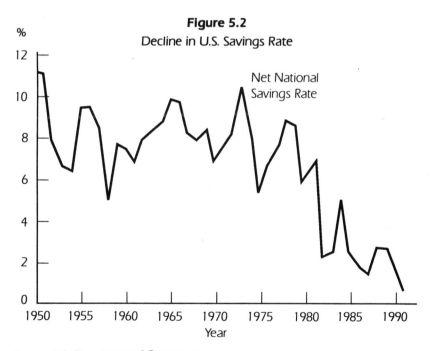

**Figure 5.2**
Decline in U.S. Savings Rate

Source: U.S. Department of Commerce

## THE 10 PERCENT SOLUTION

We strongly recommend that you begin with a 10 percent savings plan. Many of today's financial counselors emphasize a 10 percent solution; the concept was even followed by the Babylonians, the Hebrews, the Chinese and many other cultures. Ten percent is a golden number when it comes to saving. But why?

First, it's easy to figure. If your paycheck is $2,235 a month, you should save $223.50 a month. If your retirement income is $1,935 a month, put aside $193.50.

Second, it's affordable. Even a college student on a $50 weekly allowance can afford to save 10 percent, simply by forgoing a movie, or a cheeseburger and a milkshake. No one should be considered exempt from saving.

Third, it's regular. The key to building wealth is to have a consistent savings program. Pay yourself 10 percent every time you are paid. Once this plan becomes a regular part of your business life, it will be very easy and convenient to keep it going.

## IS 10 PERCENT ENOUGH?

Is a 10 percent savings plan sufficient to achieve financial security? The answer is a resounding yes!

The average American will earn approximately $1 million in a lifetime. By saving just 10 percent of that, a base sum of $100,000 will accrue. Moreover, if that $100,000 is invested wisely, and dividends and interest are reinvested, those savings will increase substantially.

Suppose you put aside $200 a month in a savings program that earns an average 10 percent annual return. How much would you have in 5, 10, 20 or 30 years? Your savings will increase dramatically. If you save $15,000 in 5 years, you'll have enough for a down payment on a house, or for other investments. In 10 years, your savings will amount to over $40,000. After 20 years, they will be over $150,000. And 30 years from now, you will have set aside $72,000, but you'll be worth nearly half a million dollars! Whether you retire in 5 years or 30 years, you will have a sizeable nest egg. And remember the example we gave in Chapter 1—the person who in 1981 started investing only $100 a month in our recommended mutual fund (Twentieth Century Select Investors) would have over $40,000 today.

You may say, "Sure, but what will $40,000 be worth 10 years from now, with inflation?" There are several ways to protect yourself from inflation when you use the 10 percent solution.

First, your 10 percent savings plan is automatically indexed to inflation. By that we mean that when you get an increase in income, the amount you save increases accordingly. Use inflation to your advantage by continuing to pay yourself 10 percent of your total income level, no matter how high it goes.

But the most important way to hedge against inflation is to invest wisely to keep your savings from losing ground. Read on for several specific recommendations that will not only make your savings program systematic and convenient but will be profitable investments as well.

# CHAPTER 6

---

# The Principles of Financial Success

*Any fool can waste, any fool can muddle, but it takes
something of a man to save, and the more he saves the
more of a man does it make of him.*

—RUDYARD KIPLING

THE STORY IS TOLD of a man who went into a hardware store to
purchase a strongbox with a sturdy combination lock. He asked
that a slit be cut into the top, as in a child's piggy bank, so that he
could slide money into the box without opening the lid. Satisfied
with the results, he picked up the box and turned to leave. "Wait a
minute, sir," the sales clerk said. "You forgot to take the combination for the lock." "Keep it," the man replied. "I always set aside
ten percent of my income, regular as clockwork, on the day I get
paid. But at the end of the month something always comes up and
I end up using the money. I want to put my money where I know I
can't get at it!"

You may not need to take such drastic measures in order to
preserve your savings, but this story does demonstrate one of the
three important principles that will help you maintain a long-term
savings program. They are:

- Make it easy to build wealth.

- Make it difficult to withdraw your savings.

- Invest your savings wisely and productively.

Let's see why each of these three steps is so essential.

## PRINCIPLE 1: MAKE IT EASY TO BUILD WEALTH

First of all, in order to save on a consistent basis you must make it *convenient and painless.*

You could write a check every time you get paid, and deposit it into your savings account or investment program. Many people use this approach, with varying degrees of success.

The drawback to this simple approach is that it requires you to make a decision every time you get paid. If you receive a paycheck every two weeks, you'll need to write a check to deposit into your savings or investment plan at least twice a month. That means making an investment decision 26 times a year! On many occasions, you might be strongly tempted to delay or miss a payment to your savings. Emergencies and unexpected bills come up frequently, and you may find yourself short of cash on payday. It is all too easy to give up on your savings plan when more immediate needs seem to be pressing on you. It may not even be a conscious decision not to save—you simply keep putting off writing the check until the money is gone and the decision is made for you. In this case, not deciding is the same as deciding "no"!

Fortunately, there are a number of alternatives that can make it easy and convenient for you to deposit your savings regularly.

### Automatic Payroll Deductions

The best way to begin a long-term savings plan is through an automatic payroll deduction program where you work. Companies already withhold money from your paycheck for taxes,

Social Security, medical insurance, etc. In addition, many employers may, with your approval, withhold for other investments made on your behalf—to purchase company stock, U.S. Savings Bonds, annuities, credit union savings accounts or mutual funds, for example.

In most cases, all you have to do is instruct your payroll department to begin withholding a specified amount from your paycheck and tell them where you would like your money to be placed. In the future, that amount will be withheld from your paycheck and deposited in your savings or investment program until you instruct them to do otherwise. It's all done automatically.

Payroll deduction savings programs are very popular among employees of major corporations. Studies have shown that those who use an automatic deduction plan tend to save more than those who don't. Why? Because this is an easy way to save.

The advantages are tremendous.

First, you take only one action. Instead of having to make 26 decisions to save each year, with a payroll deduction program you need alert your bank only once. In the future, your company will take the action for you—automatically.

Second, automatic payroll deduction is a painless way to save. There is an old saying in the finance industry, "You don't spend money you don't see." If your savings are withheld from your paycheck, you won't miss the money as much. We once spoke with a woman who said she just couldn't seem to save any money—she always spent her entire paycheck. On examining her records for her we discovered that she had an automatic savings program with her employer, who was investing nearly 25 percent of her income! Her savings program was so painless she had forgotten all about it.

Third, payroll deduction does not require a big investment. There usually is no minimum investment required to begin a payroll deduction plan, and most companies will allow employees to withhold as little as $50 a paycheck. As you can see, there is simply no excuse not to start right away, no matter how small your wage or salary may be.

Fourth, payroll deduction allows you to "dollar-cost-average" your investment. If you invest $200 a month in a market that fluctuates a great deal, you'll average out the dips and rises in the market. When prices are up, you'll buy less of the item. If prices drop, you are able to buy more units. Dollar-cost-averaging takes away the second-guessing required for short-term markets.

Fifth, many companies offer IRS-approved retirement plans, such as 401(k) plans, which allow you to invest part of your salary automatically in a tax-deferred investment plan, choosing from a variety of mutual funds. Some companies will match part or all of your investment, giving you an instant return. We strongly recommend 401(k) plans and other automatic investment programs.

Sixth, a payroll deduction plan can help you get out of debt. The same principle that makes it easy to save can make it easy to pay bills. Credit counselors often recommend using a payroll deduction program, particularly if the company credit union is handling the repayment of loans through debt consolidation. Thus, payroll deduction can be an *easy, convenient* way to pay off debts.

## Automatic Investments Through Your Checking Account

Payroll deductions are the most convenient way to save because you never see the money in the first place. However, if your company doesn't offer the variety of investments that you are looking for, or if you are self-employed, you can still take advantage of the convenience of "automatic purchase plans." You can arrange with a mutual fund, insurance company or other financial institution to have a certain amount of money automatically withdrawn from your checking account on a predetermined basis and deposited in the investment of your choice. The arrangement is simple. You provide a voided copy of a check and sign a statement authorizing the mutual fund or other organization to withdraw a specified amount by bank draft every month or every quarter. Figure out how much 10 percent of your salary or wage is and authorize that amount. If you're self-employed, take out whatever you think will represent 10 percent of your profits. You can start with as little as $50 a month. Best of all, everything is done for you.

One of our recommended mutual fund families, the Twentieth Century Group, offers this service. You can have as little as $25 a month transferred automatically from your checking account to one of their funds (such as Twentieth Century Select Investors). Call Twentieth Century Investors at 800–345–2021. The Janus Group is another recommended mutual fund family that offers this service. Normally, the minimum to open an account with Janus is $1,000, but by signing up for their automatic investment plan, you can begin by investing only $50 a month. Call Janus at 800–525–3713.

If you're retired, you can have your Social Security or pension check deposited directly into your investment account. We strongly recommend this approach for retirees who have other pension sources to live on, to provide a protection against inflation and other uncertainties.

## PRINCIPLE 2: MAKE IT DIFFICULT TO WITHDRAW YOUR SAVINGS

The next step is just as important. You may have built up a considerable savings program, but if it is too easy to withdraw your money, you may spend it all too soon on some unexpected need or emergency. When you see your wealth accumulating, possibly for the first time in your life, it can be very tempting to use it right away. If this has been a problem for you in the past, you may want to make it difficult to withdraw your savings. When you choose an investment that imposes penalties for early withdrawal, or if it requires some extra effort to sell an investment, you will be less likely to withdraw it until there is a real need. You won't waste your money on something that has no lasting value to you.

What kind of penalties or obstacles should you look for? Consider the following:

1. *Commissions or fees for withdrawals.* Many investments such as stocks, bonds, coins, collectibles and real estate require you to

pay sizeable commissions or fees if you want to liquidate. When these investments are allowed to grow for the long term, the fees are negligible. But they will help prevent you from making short-term withdrawals.

2. *Penalties for premature withdrawals.* Bank certificates of deposit, annuities, brokerage mutual funds and other investments impose substantial penalties if you withdraw your money before a predetermined time has elapsed.

3. *Taxes on profits.* If you sell an investment that has increased in value, your profits will be taxable. But your "paper profits" are not taxed until you actually sell. Potential tax liabilities can be a strong incentive to hold on, especially when you consider that Uncle Sam takes 28 percent of your profits—money you will never see again.

4. *Potential for future appreciation.* Many investors will be reluctant to sell an investment during a bull market that appears likely to continue rising in the near future.

5. *Liquidity.* Certain investments are more difficult to sell than others, because it may take a while to find a buyer. Real estate, for example, often takes weeks or months to sell. Many collectibles are also illiquid.

6. *Inconvenience.* Many investments are simply inconvenient to sell. It may take time and effort on the part of the owner before a sale can take place. You may have to take your antiques or coins to an auction to get the best price, or you may have to package them up and ship them across the country. If you deal with a full-service broker, you may have to do some talking to convince him that now is the time to sell—without making another purchase through him to replace it.

Of course, not everyone needs to take these precautions, nor should "illiquidity" be your prime consideration in choosing an investment. In fact, for short-term savings, these are the kinds of penalties you should avoid. Some people are very strong-willed and may not need to have any barriers to their savings withdrawals. But our experience has shown that most people need an incentive to keep their savings where it is. It's incredible how many situations come up where people think they need to use their savings, but when they wait it out they find other solutions to their short-term problems. Fees and penalties are often necessary to keep savings intact for as long as possible.

## Form an Investment Club

Nothing teaches like experience, and nothing motivates like having a partner. The way to achieve both while risking a relatively small amount of money is to start an investment club.

Many investors join local investment clubs as an easy way to save and invest on a steady basis. Thousands of clubs have been established over the years through the National Association of Investors Corporation (NAIC).

Investment clubs have been around for decades. Part of that popularity comes from the fact that, by pooling the resources of 15 to 25 friends, you can own a dozen stocks with as little as $25 per month.

An investment club is a good way to make little nest eggs grow. One investor joined a club in the 1950s, contributing just $20 per month. By the time he retired, he had amassed $106,000. More recently, a club of 25 women became the top-performing group in the Washington, D.C., area, averaging portfolio returns of 16 to 20 percent.

And yet you shouldn't expect to wallow in wealth after a few good stock picks. Building a profitable stock portfolio through an investment club may take a couple of years. Those clubs that turn dimes into dollars do so because their members study hard to select the right stocks. They spend time at the library looking up a stock's performance and evaluating a company's worth. If you have the time and patience to do this, forming an investment club may be profitable.

Choosing the right mix of people will play a large part in the success of your club. It's very important that your members share the same investment strategy. You would not want a group interested in aggressive growth stocks pitted against blue-chip conservatives. Squabbles over investment strategy have put many clubs out of business, although waning interest is the chief reason why most of them fail.

It is usually better to start your own club than to join an existing one because many existing clubs charge new members stiff initiation dues. Starting your own club is not difficult to do, according to the NAIC.

The club should follow three general principles:

- Invest a set sum of money regularly over a long period of time. Most clubs require members to contribute as little as $25 a month.

- Reinvest all dividends from stocks and bonds.

- Invest in growth stocks—companies that promise to be more valuable in the near future.

Many investment clubs have done extremely well over the years, often exceeding the return of top mutual funds. Other clubs, of course, have been badly hurt by bear markets or poor investment decisions. Be sure to study the investment philosophy of the other club members to ensure that they conform to your way of thinking.

If you are interested in knowing more about investment clubs, write or call:

National Association of
    Investors Corporation
1515 E. Eleven Mile Rd.
Royal Oak, MI 48067
313-543-0612

For $32 you will receive the *Investors Manual*, a handbook outlining how to organize a club, choose stocks and deal with the IRS. In addition, NAIC makes over 100 stocks available to its members with no commissions.

## PRINCIPLE 3: INVEST YOUR SAVINGS
## WISELY AND PRODUCTIVELY

Before choosing an investment program, evaluate your personal needs. Your temperament, stage of life, income level and investment knowledge all play a role in determining how you should invest. If you are retired or living on a fixed income, you can't afford to take big risks with your investment funds. Similarly, if you are just starting out and have very little knowledge or experience, you could waste all of your money in risky speculations before you gain the skills to invest wisely. Moreover, if you are the type who lies awake nights worrying about your investments, you simply don't have the emotional fortitude for the roller-coaster ride that investing can turn out to be.

There are three major categories of investment personalities. Which type are you?

1. *The traditional saver.* The traditional saver is more concerned with preserving capital than with making big gains. Retirees, widows and those on fixed incomes who need greater safety fit into this category. Usually, novice investors do, too.

While the traditional saver can sleep well during a period of low inflation, stable prices and a growing economy, low interest rates can be a real drawback. Even traditional savers must also be aware of alternative investments so they can switch some funds into higher-yielding vehicles when the economy changes.

2. *The conservative investor, or moderate risk-taker.* These investors are usually in the middle-income years, with a family, education and retirement to plan for. They can't afford to take too many risks, but they want more out of their investments than a guaranteed 5 to 10 percent return.

3. *The speculator.* Some people just starting out can afford to take greater risks, knowing that their high-income years are still ahead of them and they have that as a safeguard should they make a mistake and lose it all now. Other investors simply enjoy

the thrill of the gamble. Still others have an uncanny knack for choosing the right stock or commodity. If you have a gambler's spirit, a conservative base to fall back on and a good amount of knowledge and expertise, you would probably do well as a speculator.

If you are a speculator married to a conservative, or a conservative married to a speculator, don't despair! We often hear from investors who ask, "How can I get my spouse to show an interest in money management?" when what they really mean is "How can I get my spouse to agree with me?" But we have found that there is no single correct way to invest. In fact, differences in temperament or opinion, if treated as strengths, can lead to greater success. The most successful business people do not surround themselves with "yes" men but seek out partners and advisers who bring fresh, new ideas and outlooks. While investment disagreements can be a problem when a couple argues over who's right and who's wrong, they can also be the basis of a great team effort when viewed as separate strengths. "Divide and conquer" is a good team motto. For example, if a wife is more comfortable with traditional investments, she should be in charge of the investments that will provide your portfolio's conservative foundation. If the husband finds joy and success in speculating, let him be in charge of finding high-yield deals. By working together on choosing the moderate risks—real estate, blue-chip stocks, etc.—and by having frequent planning sessions together, you can learn from each other, and your investment success will increase. Above all, avoid a spirit of competition. Diversity can be the basis of a great partnership.

## HOW TO BUILD A BALANCED PORTFOLIO

Have you ever watched a child trying to balance in the center of a teeter-totter? His weight pushes the board first one way, then the other, as he endeavors to remain in the center with both ends up.

The slightest imbalance in either direction will cause the board to fall, and so will the child.

Contrast this, however, with a child playing at the top of a hill. She can hop on one foot, stand on her head, take all kinds of risks, while remaining quite safe atop her firm foundation.

Creating a balanced portfolio is not unlike these two examples. Many investors start out trying to keep the teeter-totter aloft, investing in numerous high-risk speculations with only the barest minimum in down-to-earth, feet-on-the-ground investments. In our travels, we have met numerous people who have a dozen investments in penny stocks, rare coins, oil wells and movie deals, without a single conservative investment to buffer any losses. When these speculations don't work out (and most of them don't), investors have no liquid secure assets to fall back on.

One fellow felt he had a sure deal in silver futures a couple of years ago. He bought all he could on margin (borrowing money from the brokerage firm), expecting the price to rise quickly. When the price fell instead and he received a margin call, requiring him to put up additional cash or forfeit his entire investment, he put up more money. When the next margin call came, he enjoined a friend to participate in the "sure deal." Eventually, of course, his precarious position collapsed, all his money disappeared and his friend went down with him.

This does not mean you should avoid speculative investments altogether, however. There are many valuable profits to be made in high-risk territory, and there is a safe, conservative way to speculate. It begins by creating a portfolio pyramid. Just as the child atop the solid hill felt confident to play, so will you gain confidence and safety by creating a portfolio with a solid foundation.

The secret is to make sure that your conservative investments outweigh your speculative ones. Begin by dividing your investments into three categories: conservative, moderately risky and speculative. Specific items will probably change categories from time to time, as investment climate changes. For example, right now a stock mutual fund is a fairly conservative investment, while in the mid-1970s it was considered a speculation (or downright foolish). Similarly, mining shares were once moderately risky during the 1970s, but they are highly speculative today.

• *The conservative foundation.* Investments in this category would include interest-bearing accounts such as money market funds and certificates of deposit; high-quality corporate bonds that you intend to hold to maturity; cash value insurance products with a solid insurance company; Treasury securities; and good-quality municipal bonds.

• *The moderate risks.* Some of these investments might overlap the other two categories, depending on economic factors, specific characteristics and your debt position. They include blue-chip stocks, top-rated mutual funds, growth stocks, zero-coupon bonds, utilities, Ginnie Maes, bullion coins, rental properties with positive cash flow, second mortgages and your own business.

• *Speculative investments.* This category could include almost anything—limited partnerships, penny mining stocks, aggressive growth stocks, commodities, futures, foreign stocks and currencies, rare coins, new issues, highly leveraged real estate, options, warrants, you name it. These investments are exciting, with a hint of danger as well as the promise of high profits. You can get rich overnight—or you could lose it all just as quickly.

Next, determine what percentage of your portfolio falls into each category. Then draw a bar graph for yourself, putting your conservative investments at the bottom, your moderately risky investments centered above that, and your speculative investments at the top. The shape of the resultant configuration should tell you whether your portfolio is top-heavy, weighted down sluggishly or well-balanced. What does your pyramid look like? Does it resemble a Coke bottle, a wrestler's chest or the tomb of an ancient pharaoh? Could you perch comfortably atop it, or would you feel precariously unbalanced?

## THE INVESTMENT PYRAMID

There is no single perfect portfolio mix. Consideration of age, temperament, knowledge and income must be taken into account.

Generally, however, we would expect a middle-aged, middle-income, reasonably skillful investor to have an equilateral pyramid (Figure 6.1), with perhaps 50 percent invested conservatively, 30 percent in moderately risky investments and 20 percent in speculations.

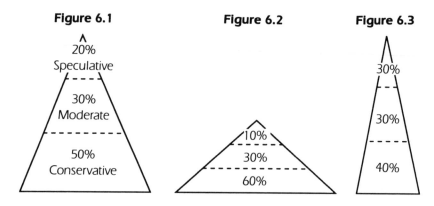

Figure 6.1

20%
Speculative

30%
Moderate

50%
Conservative

Figure 6.2

10%
30%
60%

Figure 6.3

30%

30%

40%

Someone on a fixed income, retired or with little experience with investing should have a flatter pyramid (Figure 6.2), with a broad base of at least 60 percent conservative investments, 30 percent moderate risks and no more than 10 percent speculations.

A person who is under 50, with a high income and several years of skillful experience, could have a pyramid resembling the Washington monument (Figure 6.3), with perhaps 40 percent in conservative investments, 30 percent in moderate risks, and 30 percent in high flyers.

### What if the Top Topples?

The purpose of this pyramid plan is to provide a safety net, not a pocketbook. If the silver speculator dips into his moderately risky investments to cover his first margin call, and then into his conservative base to cover his second margin call, he loses the whole point (and the rest of the pyramid, too).

If a speculation goes sour and you lose money, stay out of that market until you have saved enough *new income* to reenter it. Your speculating money is money you can afford to lose, but your foundation money is not. Never throw good money after bad.

On the other hand, if a speculation does very well and you double or triple your investment, the pyramid approach will guide you to lock in some profits. Too many investors rejoice as they watch their pyramids inflate at the top, then curse their bad luck when it invariably deflates again. Paper profits mean nothing until you place a sell order.

If you use this balanced approach to investing, you will be able to increase your skills, enjoy high-yielding profits and still feel a sense of security. You can turn cartwheels at the top of the hill.

# CHAPTER 7

# Your High-Yielding Investment Account

*There are three faithful friends—an old wife, an old dog, and ready money.*

—Poor Richard's Almanac

$W$HILE THE REAL PROFITS may be made today in the more sophisticated areas of stocks, foreign investments, real estate and other long-term investments, you still need a place to put your short-term cash. You need a short-term savings plan, to be drawn on when unexpected expenses come up. You also need a place to "park" your long-term savings or investment funds from time to time, while waiting for changes in the investment outlook. Ideally, you should have two separate accounts for these two purposes, so that the funds do not mix. But where should you place these short-term savings for maximum liquidity and maximum yield?

Prior to the financial revolution of the 1970s, upper-income investors had an advantage over small investors. With a minimum of $100,000, they could earn superior yields from jumbo certificates of deposit. With $25,000 or more, they could invest in such exotic vehicles as banker's acceptances, commercial paper,

Eurodollar deposits, adjustable rate mortgages or money market certificates. With $10,000 or more, they could buy Treasury bills directly from the U.S. Treasury. In every case, the minimum investment was far beyond the pocketbook of any small investor.

Fortunately, all that changed during the 1970s. The deregulation of the financial services industry brought us money market funds, cash management accounts and other vehicles for investors of all sizes to earn the highest yields possible with very low minimums.

Today there are a wide variety of choices where all investors, large or small, can park their money and earn high income while waiting for another investment opportunity. Let us consider some of them.

## THE MONEY FUNDS

Most people have heard of money market funds. These are mutual funds that pool the resources of thousands of investors to take advantage of high yields on Treasury bills, large bank CDs, commercial paper and so forth. With mutual funds, the high minimums required for individual investments are spread among a number of smaller investors, so that you don't need to have $10,000 or more to get started.

The advantages of money market funds are these:

• *Potentially high yields.* Money funds earned nearly 17 percent during the 1980–81 credit squeeze, although ten years later they were paying 5 percent or less. Still, they usually give a better return than the passbook rate at savings institutions.

• *No load.* "Load" is another term for the commissions charged by some mutual funds. With money funds, you don't have to pay a broker a commission. One hundred percent of your money goes to work earning high returns right away.

- *Low minimum investment.* You don't have to have a fortune to begin investing—most funds require just $1,000, and some funds have no minimum.
- *No penalty for withdrawal.* You don't have to wait until maturity to collect on the money fund investments. You don't even have to wait for a refund to be sent. Just write a check.
- *Check-writing privileges.* Withdrawing your money is simple, using the free checks the fund sends you to redeem your "shares." Thus, money funds are like interest-bearing checking accounts. Many funds require you to write a check for at least $250, however.
- *Ease and convenience.* Most funds offer a toll-free number to call for information or to open an account. You can also track the weekly return on all funds in the Monday edition of *The Wall Street Journal.*

Money market funds are not insured by the federal government. This means that, while we don't expect any money funds to fail, your principal cannot be guaranteed. However, money market funds protect themselves by diversifying their investments. They are required by law to have no more than 5 percent in any one investment, and in practice they seldom put more than 2 percent in a single vehicle. Consequently, even if one of the investments failed entirely—an unlikely event—it would affect only 2 percent of the fund's total investments. In short, they are safe.

## Recommended Money Funds

You'll find that the yields differ from one money fund to another because each fund invests in a different variety of money market instruments. We recommend the following funds for their low minimums, stability and good service.

| Name | Minimum | 1992 Yield | Minimum Check-Writing Privilege |
|------|---------|------------|---------------------------------|
| Twentieth Century Cash Reserve<br>P.O. Box 419200<br>Kansas City, MO 64141<br>800-345-2021 | $ 0 | 2.6% | $500 |
| New England Cash Mgmt. Trust<br>399 Boylston St.<br>Boston, MA 02115<br>800-343-7104 | $ 25 | 3.1% | $250 |
| MIMLIC Money Market Fund<br>400 N. Roberts St.<br>St. Paul, MN 55101<br>800-443-3677 | $250 | 2.8% | $250 |
| Daily Cash Accumulation<br>3410 South Galena St.<br>Denver, CO 80231<br>800-525-7048 | $500 | 3.2% | $250 |

Source: *IBC/Donoghue's Money Fund Directory* ($29.95)
     P.O. Box 91004, Ashland, WA 01721, 800-343-5413

The Twentieth Century money fund is part of the Twentieth Century family of funds. Twentieth Century is an ideal fund family for the small investor—the minimum for all its investments is zero! We will have more to say about this great fund family in Chapter 8.

## BANK MONEY MARKET ACCOUNTS

Commercial banks and savings institutions offer *money market accounts* to compete with money market funds. They are convenient and are insured up to $100,000 by the federal government. But they are not as flexible as money funds. Check-writing privileges are more limited, for example.

## CASH MANAGEMENT ACCOUNTS

All major brokerage firms offer *cash management accounts*, similar to money market funds with check-writing privileges. When you open a brokerage account, you can place your funds in a cash management account, which allows you to earn interest income immediately while you decide where to invest your money. When you sell a stock, bond or other investment, you can transfer the money to your cash management account instead of having the proceeds of the sale sent to you, where you might be tempted to spend it. Most brokerage firms offer a choice of three funds or more—a taxable money fund, a tax-free money fund, and an all-government fund. Cash management accounts are probably the most flexible of all cash accounts. You can use your account to write checks in any amount, to buy stocks, bonds and mutual funds, and to take advantage of a debit card offered by the brokerage firm (usually through MasterCard or Visa).

For more information, contact a local branch of Merrill Lynch, Shearson Lehman Brothers, Prudential Securities, PaineWebber or any major brokerage house. Discount brokerage firms such as Charles Schwab & Co. also offer CMAs.

## PRIME-RATE FUNDS AND ADJUSTABLE-RATE FUNDS

Due to a decline in yields on money funds and CDs in the early 1990s to under 4 percent, the financial services industry has come up with several alternatives that offer superior yields.

*Prime-rate funds* are, as their name suggests, funds linked to the prime rate, the interest charged by large commercial banks to their favorite customers. In early 1992, the rate was 6.5 percent, while passbook accounts were paying a dismal 4 percent. The prime-rate funds attempt to pay a rate equivalent to the prime rate. The yield varies with the prime rate, while the principal tends to stay relatively stable. Prime-rate funds are available from

Merrill Lynch, Allstate, and the Pilgrim Prime Rate Fund, which trades on the New York Stock Exchange.

Adjustable-rate mortgage funds invest in adjustable-rate mortgages on the secondary market, and were paying around 6 to 7 percent in early 1992. Adjustable-rate funds are less volatile than long-term bonds because the yield varies rather than the principal. Since these funds have become available, they have yielded an average two percentage points more than money funds and T-bills, while maintaining a fairly stable net asset value.

One of the most popular funds has been the Adjustable Rate Mortgage Fund, managed by the Benham Group of Funds, 1665 Charleston Rd., Mountain View, CA 94043, 800-472-3389. Minimum investment is $1,000, and a check-writing privilege is available.

## SHORT-TERM GLOBAL INCOME FUNDS

Another alternative growing in popularity is short-term global income funds. These funds invest in foreign money market instruments, including Euro certificates of deposit and short-term bonds. They take advantage of higher interest rates in Europe and the Far East. For example, while U.S. dollar accounts might be paying 4 to 6 percent, the British pound, German mark or Japanese yen might be paying 8 to 10 percent. Global income funds allow you to invest in a variety of currencies without having to open a foreign bank account.

The major risk of these funds is the volatile currency exchange. If the dollar falls against major currencies, the fund's value rises. But if the dollar rallies, the fund will decline in value. The principal is not guaranteed to remain stable as it is for money funds.

One fund that has attempted to hedge the currency risk is the Blanchard Short-Term Global Income Fund. The yield has generally been three to four percentage points higher than money funds and T-bills, and the net asset value has fluctuated only slightly so far. For more information, contact the Blanchard

Group of Funds, 41 Madison Ave., 24th floor, New York, NY 10010, 800-922-7771. Minimum investment is $3,000, and a check-writing privilege is available.

## YOU CAN EARN HIGH INTEREST ON YOUR CASH

There are many alternatives available to the small investor who wants to earn high income on short-term money. Whether it be money market funds, money market accounts, cash management accounts, prime-rate funds, adjustable-rate funds or global income funds, you can earn interest income every day with your parked funds. Get started today!

# CHAPTER 8

---

# Low-Risk, Low-Cost Investing in the Stock Market

*No gains without pains.*

—Poor Richard's Almanac

THE STOCK MARKET IS the most popular means in the world of investing in free enterprise. Thousands of companies of every size are traded on the New York Stock Exchange, the American Stock Exchange, regional exchanges and on NASDAQ. Add to that the thousands of foreign stocks trading on foreign exchanges around the world, and you can easily see why the stock market is the most liquid trading market in the world of finance.

It used to be difficult for the small investor to play the stock market. The small investor had to pay extra for "odd" lot purchases of fewer than 100 shares, and the minimums on managed accounts were high. Small investors have always been intimidated by the big brokerage outfits.

But now that's all changed. Some top-performing mutual funds allow you to invest without paying a commission and with very little minimum—sometimes no minimum at all. And a new development now allows you to buy fractional shares of blue-chip companies without a commission. The minimum in one case is only one share! This chapter tells you all about it.

## CHOOSING STOCKS FOR SAFETY, GROWTH AND PROFIT

Before you begin investing in the stock market, you should familiarize yourself with the variety of stocks available. There are numerous kinds of stocks, as well as several stock exchanges available. You should also examine your own investment personality so you'll pick a stock portfolio with which you can be comfortable.

In the next pages we'll discuss the various categories of stocks. Here's how they perform in general and who should invest in them.

### Blue-Chip Stocks

These are the safest stocks you can buy and are often chosen by retirees, trust managers and others who can't afford to take big risks. They feature higher dividend yields than most common stocks, making them very attractive to those who need investment income for living expenses.

"Blue-chip" generally refers to the major multimillion-dollar corporations traded on the New York Stock Exchange, the ones that have been around for years and are likely to remain for years more. All of the 30 stocks that make up the Dow Jones Industrial Average would be considered blue-chips, including American Telephone and Telegraph, Exxon, DuPont, GM, McDonald's, IBM, Procter & Gamble, Eastman Kodak, General Electric, Sears, Coca-Cola and Disney (see Figure 8.1).

Blue-chips may not be exciting, but they tend to be the most stable and safe.

**Figure 8.1**

Blue-Chip Stocks, 1982–1992

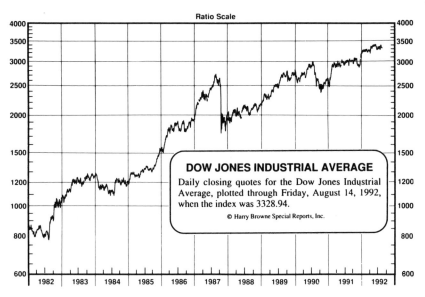

DOW JONES INDUSTRIAL AVERAGE

Daily closing quotes for the Dow Jones Industrial Average, plotted through Friday, August 14, 1992, when the index was 3328.94.

© Harry Browne Special Reports, Inc.

## Growth Stocks

While blue-chip companies can emphasize stable earnings, growth stocks emphasize capital appreciation. These companies are expanding rapidly and consequently need to reinvest earnings. Some examples of growth industries in recent decades would include companies developing computers, drugs, aerospace equipment, electronics, cosmetics and office equipment. Growth stocks are more suitable for investors who are looking for long-term growth rather than current income. They are more risky because they may not have a long-term track record, and there is no guarantee that consumer demand for the product will make it a household item or that cheap competition won't drive the original developers out of business.

## Penny Stocks

Penny stocks get their name from the fact that they sell for pennies rather than dollars. Investors in these companies buy shares of a brand-new company, whose product may be new or unproven. They are always highly speculative and extremely risky. For every penny stock that doubles or triples in value, more than a hundred others never go anywhere, and investors in those companies can lose a lot.

This is not to say that you should never invest in pennies. There might be a new invention that you personally believe in, or you may know a stockbroker who has an amazing track record. But a general rule of thumb when investing in pennies is to buy a basketful, hoping one will be a winner to offset the losers.

## Utility Stocks

Unlike most companies operating in the free market, utility companies are awarded a monopoly or partial monopoly to provide water, electricity, gas and telephone service within an area. They are regulated by state agencies and, significantly, are allowed to charge rates that usually guarantee them a fair rate of return. Because of this guaranteed profit, many money managers recommend that a portion of their clients' portfolios be in utilities as a safe and profitable investment.

## PLAYING THE STOCK EXCHANGES

There are more than a dozen exchanges in this country alone that offer stocks for sale. Does it matter which one you use?

In dollar volume, about 60 percent of all stock market business is traded on the New York Stock Exchange (NYSE), also known as the "Big Board." There are more than 2,500 stocks listed on the NYSE, and in order for a company to be listed, it must fulfill several stringent requirements. Most of the companies listed on the NYSE exceed these requirements by a wide margin, but they may have had to get their start on another exchange before being large enough to qualify for the Big Board.

While the New York Stock Exchange (NYSE) is unquestionably the largest in terms of volume, it is not necessarily the only one to use. In fact, in recent years the NYSE has lost some of its customer share, moving from an 85 percent share of the total market in 1960 to the current 60 percent.

The American Stock Exchange (AMEX) is also located in New York. Many blue-chip stocks, including General Motors and Standard Oil, got their start on the AMEX before switching to the Big Board. All of the nation's major brokerage firms maintain seats on the AMEX, as well as on the NYSE.

There are numerous other regional exchanges, including the Midwest Stock Exchange in Chicago, the Pacific Stock Exchange and the Philadelphia Stock Exchange. All regional exchanges specialize in the growth companies located within their particular geographic areas.

Because they don't have the size and volume requirements imposed by the New York Stock Exchange, the regional exchanges are more likely to have newly issued stocks, small growth companies, local utilities and other stocks that have greater growth potential than the larger, well-established companies. Many of them carry the Big Board stocks as well.

All of these exchanges are registered with the Securities and Exchange Commission (SEC) and must adhere strictly to specific regulations.

The fastest-growing exchange is NASDAQ, the so-called "over the counter" market. Unlike the established exchanges, where brokers go to a specific location to buy and sell, NASDAQ is actually a complex system of nationwide computer hookups and communications networks that links thousands of securities firms to one another. NASDAQ also trades bonds, government securities and shares in foreign companies.

Be aware that commissions and bid-asked spreads vary when dealing with NASDAQ stocks. The cost between buying and selling a stock might vary by 10 percent or more in cases of illiquid stocks, meaning that the stock must increase by at least that much for you to break even, let alone make a profit.

## Foreign Stock Exchanges

There are other stock exchanges around the world that sell stocks of companies in foreign countries. For example, Canada has five very active exchanges, the largest of which is in Toronto. These exchanges specialize mostly in Canadian stocks, of course, but in recent years the Canadian exchanges have become a popular place for new American companies to get their start because Canada's filing requirements are much less stringent and less costly than those in the United States.

When purchasing a foreign stock on a U.S. stock exchange, you'll receive an American Depository Receipt (ADR), which is a certificate verifying that you have shares in a foreign stock and that they are deposited in the foreign office of an American bank or in one of its correspondent banks abroad.

Many seasoned investors like to speculate on foreign exchanges because they can actually profit in two ways: The stock can rise in price, and the foreign currency in which it is denominated can also rise. Of course, it works both ways: If the dollar is strengthening, you could lose money overall, even if the stock itself does well. Approach these markets with caution.

Investing in foreign stocks and mutual funds can be extremely profitable. See Chapter 11 in this book for specific guidelines.

## HOW TO CHOOSE A WINNING STOCK

There are many successful methods for choosing stocks. Some people rely heavily on price/earnings (P/E) ratios. Others study a company's annual reports, assets and liabilities, product development and competition. Still others prefer the exactness of technical charts and "moving averages." All of these methods require a great deal of time and study.

New investors often feel more comfortable relying on the expertise of others who have been picking stocks for a long time. A stockbroker can be a good source of information, but if you prefer to research your own stock picks, we recommend the quiet, anonymous and valuable information compiled by *Value Line Investment Survey* (711 Third Ave., New York, NY 10017, $525 a year). Fortunately, you don't have to pay $525 to get *Value Line*. Most public libraries carry it.

*Value Line* is a weekly publication that provides the subscriber with a detailed analysis of the market, including a look at Washington, the Federal Reserve, foreign influences and general market conditions. It grades more than 1,700 different stocks with regard to timeliness (a stock's profit potential over the next 12 months based on its current price) and safety, and prints each stock's prices, P/E ratio, expected yield, long-term potential, dividend history and industry rank. *Value Line* also profiles a specific company in each issue.

We find such fundamental analysis to be extremely valuable in choosing a stock.

If you invest in individual stocks, you will want to monitor their progress without having to call your broker each day. *The Wall Street Journal* or your local business section is a good source. But reading the stock listings can be intimidating to first-time investors. What do all the little numbers mean?

Let's examine a sample stock listing. It might look something like this:

| 52 Weeks | | | | Yld | P/E | Sales | | | | |
|---|---|---|---|---|---|---|---|---|---|---|
| High | Low | Stock | Div. | % | Ratio | 100s | High | Low | Close | Net Chg. |
| 10 1/4 | 58 1/2 | Marriot | .44 | .6 | 16 | 176 | 75 1/2 | 74 3/4 | 75 1/4 | + 1/4 |

The first two figures give the highest and lowest selling prices for the preceding year, and can be helpful in seeing how stable the stock has been.

The next two numbers show that the last dividend paid 44 cents per share and that it represented a yield of 0.6 percent. Dividends are usually paid quarterly or semiannually, but yields are annualized to facilitate comparison.

The price/earnings ratio of sixteen is calculated by dividing price (75 1/4) by earnings-per-share (the total earnings of the company divided by the total volume of shares). A P/E ratio of 16 to 20 is considered healthy.

By multiplying the next number, 176, times 100, we get the volume of Marriott shares traded the previous day (17,600). Volume of trade can be an important indication of the stock's liquidity—you wouldn't have any trouble selling a hundred shares in a hurry in this case. Volume can also indicate whether investors are rapidly dumping or snapping up a stock. There are about 27,000,000 shares of Marriott stock, so 17,600 shares traded is nothing to get excited about.

Buying stocks is nothing like going to the grocery store; it's more like attending an auction. You never know from one minute to the next what prices are going to be. The next two numbers on the line show the high and low prices paid for the stock on the previous day, and the third number shows what the final price was at the close of the market. Again, this gives an indication of the stability of the stock.

The final column shows how much the stock gained or lost from the previous day's close. In this case, it was up 25 cents.

## HOW TO CHOOSE A STOCKBROKER

Choosing a stockbroker is one of the most important decisions you will make, aside from choosing actual stocks. You will be relying on this person to execute your orders accurately and to have a good understanding of the markets. One lapse in judgment and you could lose money. It is critical that your broker understand and respect your temperament and not try to change you from a conservative to a speculator.

Most people turn first to a full-service broker at a major investment firm because they are looking for quality, experience and dependability and expect to find it at a business that has a long-established reputation. There are several advantages to dealing with a full-service broker at such a large investment firm. For one thing, these brokers do more than execute buy and sell orders. They evaluate stocks on the basis of P/E ratio, management, company debt, past performance and other market indicators. Large brokerage houses employ analysts to study the stocks and issue lists of recommended buys and sells for their customers.

Another advantage is that, before they can begin selling securities, these (and all) stockbrokers must pass a rigorous examination administered by the NASD. Plus, stockbrokers tend to take good care of their most valued customers.

Each of these advantages comes with its disadvantages. For example, you pay for the extra services provided by full-service brokers—and the commissions can be high. Is it worth the cost? The test administered by the NASD primarily examines the brokers' understanding of securities laws, not how well they choose stocks or deal with clients. You must make that evaluation for yourself. And it may take several years, and a sizeable portfolio, for a new customer to get on the broker's valued-client list.

If you decide after all to deal with a full-service broker, you should work to get on that mental "valued" list right away. Deal with a local broker, one you can meet face-to-face, and begin to establish a genuine friendship. Test the broker's willingness to provide background information on a stock without pushing you to buy. If the broker is recommending companies you've never heard of, check *Value Line*'s rating of the stock, and ask about the fundamental factors leading to the recommendation. If you have a friend who has had a successful relationship with a stockbroker for several years, ask for an introduction. Above all, try to avoid calling a brokerage house without an introduction or the name of a specific broker. As a new customer, you will most likely be assigned to the newest broker in the firm, thus losing the advantages of quality, experience and reputation that made you seek a well-known firm in the first place.

## Discount Brokers

Discount brokers simply execute your buy and sell orders. They do not supply stock evaluations or recommendations, and they will not try to talk you into or out of the purchase of any stock. Their fees are much lower than those charged by full-service brokers, often by as much as 70 percent. Consequently, your profits begin working for you, rather than covering commissions, much sooner.

Be very careful in choosing a discount broker. Major discounters advertise in the financial newspapers such as *The Wall Street Journal* and *Barron's*. They usually offer toll-free numbers.

Here is a list of discount brokers whose services are available nationwide:

Jack White & Co.
9191 Towne Centre Dr.
Suite 220
San Diego, CA 92122
800-233-3411

Charles Schwab & Co.
101 Montgomery St.
San Francisco, CA 94104
800-648-5300
415-627-7000

Fidelity Brokerage
   Services, Inc.
82 Devonshire St.
Boston, MA 02109
800-544-7272

Marquette de Bary Co.
488 Madison Ave.
New York, NY 10022
800-221-3305

Quick & Reilly, Inc.
26 Broadway
New York, NY 10004
800-221-5220
212-943-8686

Charles Schwab & Co. has been the most aggressive of the discounters, opening offices across the country. Schwab offers a wide variety of services and is highly recommended for the investor who wants to get started with as little as $500. It was the first discount brokerage house to buy and sell no-load mutual funds at very low commissions, allowing clients to diversify their investments with just one account.

## HOW TO BUY SELECTED STOCKS WITHOUT COMMISSIONS

Would you like to buy shares of a single stock without paying commissions at all? More than 100 major companies currently offer to sell their stocks directly to shareholders without charging a broker's fee. It's part of the Low-Cost Investment Plan developed by the National Association of Investors Corporation (NAIC) mentioned in Chapter 6.

Here's how it works. You become a member of NAIC, which costs $32 a year, and form an investment "club" with just one member—you! There are no minimum membership requirements. As a one-member club, you can purchase individual shares on your own. Then you select stocks from more than 100 public companies currently available through NAIC. You can begin with a purchase of a single share if you wish. There is a one-time $5 start-up charge, but in most cases, all other costs, including commissions, are paid by the public corporation. For details contact:

National Association of
   Investors Corporation
1515 E. Eleven Mile Rd.
Royal Oak, MI 48067
313-543-0612

## VIPS—HOW TO BUY BLUE-CHIP STOCKS WITHOUT A COMMISSION AND WITH VERY LOW MINIMUMS

In the past few years, a new development has made a lot of small investors happy: Now there's a way to buy shares in hundreds of top-quality public companies without paying a commission, and with a very low minimum.

You may have heard of Dividend Reinvestment Plans, commonly called DRIPs. When you sign up for a DRIP, the company automatically reinvests all your dividends (usually paid quarterly) in additional shares without taking a commission.

Many companies that offer DRIPs now offer another super benefit—Voluntary Investment Plans, or VIPs. These allow you to buy additional shares directly from the company without paying commissions. Once you become a stockholder, you can sign up for the company's DRIP and then buy additional shares directly from the company.

Several blue-chip companies allow you to purchase your first share directly from the company: Procter & Gamble (800-742-6253; minimum one share), Exxon (800-252-1800; minimum $250) and Texaco (800-283-9785; minimum $250). You pay the same price as everyone else for your stock, but you pay virtually no commission. What a deal!

Most other companies require you to buy stock from a broker first, and then you can buy directly from the company.

Note: Every VIP and DRIP program is different. Be sure to contact each company before sending money.

For a list of companies offering this incredible VIP program, and to answer all your questions, we suggest you obtain a copy of our special report "How To Buy Stocks Commission Free," available for $10 from our newsletter, *Forecasts & Strategies*, 7811 Montrose Rd., Potomac, MD 20854, 800-777-5005.

Here are several dozen top-quality blue-chip companies that allow shareholders to buy additional shares for no commission:

| | |
|---|---|
| Abbott Laboratories | Allied Signal |
| Aetna Life & Casualty Co. | American Brands |
| Alcoa | American Express Co. |
| Allegheny Power Systems, Inc. | Anheuser-Busch |
| | ARCO |

AT&T
Atlanta Gas Light Co.
Atlantic Richfield
Baltimore Gas & Electric
Banc One Corp.
Bancorp Hawaii
Bankers Trust
Barnett Bank
Bausch & Lomb
Bell Atlantic
BellSouth
Beneficial Corp.
Boise Cascade Corp.
Borden
Bristol Myers Squibb
British Petroleum
Brooklyn Union Gas Co.
Campbell Soup Co.
Cincinnati Bell
Clorox
Coca-Cola
Colgate Palmolive
Corning, Inc.
R. R. Donnelley & Sons
Dow Chemical
Dow Jones & Co.
Duke Power
DuPont
Eastman Kodak
Exxon
Freeport McMoRan
GE
Gerber Products
Giant Food
Gillette
GTE

H. J. Heinz
Hershey Foods
Humana
IBM
Indiana Energy
Kellogg
Kimberly Clark
Knight Ridder
Johnson & Johnson
McDonald's
Merck
Mobil
J. P. Morgan
NYNEX Corp.
Oklahoma Gas & Electric
J. C. Penney
PepsiCo
Pfizer
Philip Morris
Potomac Electric Power
Procter & Gamble
Quaker Oats
SCE Corp.
Texaco
3M
Union Pacific
Upjohn
Wachovia Corp.
Walgreen
Waste Management
Weyerhaeuser
Winn-Dixie
Wisconsin Energy Corp.
Woolworth
Wrigley

## HIGH-PERFORMANCE MUTUAL FUNDS

What if you feel uncomfortable about selecting your own stocks? Mutual funds may be the answer. Mutual funds pool the money of thousands of investors in order to purchase hundreds of stocks. Each investor owns a portion of the total portfolio.

Mutual funds enjoyed a fine reputation during the 1950s and early 1960s, but in the late 1960s and early 1970s many of them fell sharply. However, a few funds have continued to make spectacular profits through bear and bull markets alike. Moreover, it is now possible to switch out of a mutual fund and into a more profitable fund or alternative investment without paying any penalty or commission. Clearly, by choosing a well-managed fund, you can still make a good profit in the stock market, without constantly monitoring your own portfolio of stock picks.

Mutual funds share many of the advantages of individual stocks. They qualify for inclusion in Individual Retirement Accounts (IRAs) and business pension plans. However, be aware that most mutual funds have annual "distributions" which may be partly taxable.

### Commission or No Commission?

There are two kinds of mutual funds—load and no-load. Load funds require the investor to pay 3 to 9 percent of the purchase price to the broker up front. This not only becomes expensive, but it begins to cloud your judgment as well, since there is a tendency to stay with the investment "until you earn your money back." It inhibits trading, which is a disadvantage because in this ever-changing economy you may want to switch investments.

No-load funds require no commissions at all—they are sold directly by the management company without the use of brokers, so 100 percent of your money goes to work.

Which is better? For the small investor, the no-loads are usually the better choice.

Studies have shown that load funds do not outperform the no-load funds. A survey of mutual funds by *Forbes* concluded: "Year after year, the *Forbes* survey has found no basis for thinking load funds do better than no-loads, or vice versa. This year as last, one-third of the funds that made *Forbes'* honor roll were no-loads."

The no-load market is booming, and 25 percent of all mutual funds are now no-loads. Their advantages are outstanding.

### Advantages of No-Load Mutual Funds

• *No sales commissions.* A full 100 percent of your money is placed in the fund. You could conceivably buy one day and sell the next, without any penalties or commissions. Any costs or administrative fees are spread out over the year, and they are figured into the value of the shares. Annual expenses are important, however, and should be watched carefully when you invest.

*Forbes* magazine conducts an annual survey of the costs and performance of mutual funds each September. You would be wise to purchase a copy. Before you invest in a fund, whether load or no-load, check *Forbes's* rating of the fund. You should also check *Morningstar's Mutual Fund Survey*, available at most libraries.

• *No broker.* How you invest, where you invest and when you invest are up to you. And since you don't have to fill out the revealing forms required by brokerage firms, you have a good deal of privacy.

• *Diversification.* The mutual fund invests in a large variety of companies, allowing you to spread the risk as well as the reward.

• *Specialization.* Many funds specialize in one particular kind of investment, such as utilities, T-bills, growth stocks, gold, foreign stocks or blue-chips. This allows you to enjoy diversification and specialization at the same time.

• *Professional management.* Now you can have the professional management that was formerly available only to wealthy investors. When you pool your financial resources with thousands of other investors, you can afford money managers who work full time investing on your behalf. When you decide to sell, you don't have to consider the merits of each individual stock, wondering if you should hang on to some and sell others. You simply sell the mutual fund. The management varies considerably from fund to fund, so this is by far the most important item to monitor when investing in mutual funds.

• *Convenience.* Many no-load mutual funds offer toll-free numbers for inquiries and even permit buying and selling by phone. The telephone-switch privilege allows you to switch into and out of no-load funds when you think the market is going to turn.

The "net asset value" (the price at which you can sell the fund) is set every day. It is published in most major newspapers around the country, including *The Wall Street Journal,* under "Mutual Funds" or "Investment Funds," so it's simple to find out how your fund is doing. But don't panic if your fund seems to drop suddenly overnight. From time to time fund managers decide to sell some of the fund's holdings, which results in a "distribution." This reduces the price of individual shares, but it does not reduce the value of your investment. Your share of the profits from the sale is reinvested, so now you have more shares than you originally purchased. Even though the price per share has dropped, your overall investment has increased.

Some investors choose to have their dividends and distributions paid to them rather than reinvested. If you select that option when you open the account, you will receive a check rather than additional shares when a distribution occurs. We believe reinvestment is much wiser than having a check sent to you because it keeps your investment growing.

Depending on what was sold, you may incur a tax consequence as a result of the distribution. You will receive a statement at the end of the year telling you exactly what your tax obligation is.

Distributions, like stock splits, are not an uncommon occurrence. They keep the individual share price at affordable levels and are necessary from time to time as market factors change and portfolio managers find it necessary to switch investments.

Dividend payments will be treated the same way, either as a reinvestment that increases your share holdings or an income check, depending on your instructions.

• *Liquidity.* You can buy or sell at any time, without penalty. You can redeem your shares by writing a letter or by calling the fund on the phone. Many funds permit withdrawal by telephone, by bank wire (whereby money is electronically transferred to your bank account) or by check.

• *Automatic purchase plans.* Many mutual funds allow you to invest automatically each month by having funds withdrawn from your checking account. This is an excellent way to guarantee that you will become richer every month, because it forces you to save. Some of the mutual funds that offer this advantage include Dreyfus, Vanguard, Fidelity, Scudders, Lexington, Financial, United Services, Templeton, Twentieth Century and International Investors.

No-load funds exist in virtually any category you may desire. There are more than 1,000 no-loads on the market today. Most of them fit into one of the following categories:

• *Growth stocks,* which emphasize price appreciation but pay little or no dividend.

• *Income funds,* which seek high dividends or interest from stocks, bonds and money market instruments and are good for those who need regular income from their investments.

• *Natural resource* and *energy funds.*

• *International funds,* which invest in foreign securities.

• *Municipal bond funds* with tax-free yields and check-writing privileges.

• *Gold share funds,* which invest in South African and North American mining shares.

- *Government bond funds.*

- *Corporate bond funds* with higher yields, monthly income.

- *Specialty funds* such as embryonic companies, technology stocks, utilities, medical companies, etc.

### How To Get Started in No-Load Funds

For a list of no-load mutual funds, write:

No-Load Mutual Funds Membership List
Investment Company Institute
1600 M St., NW, Suite 600
Washington, D.C. 20036
202-293-7700

Also, a complete list can be found in *Forbes' Annual Mutual Fund Survey*, published each September, and *Morningstar's Mutual Fund Survey*.

Minimum investment requirements vary considerably. The average minimum is $1,000.

### No Minimum Investing

There is good news for the stock market investor who is just starting out, or for students, children and others who have little money with which to begin: One management company fund has no minimum investment and has been a good long-term performer. It has been on the *Forbes* honor roll in the past. For a prospectus, write or call:

Twentieth Century Select Investors
P.O. Box 419200
Kansas City, MO 64141
800-345-2021
816-531-5575

Twentieth Century Select Investors and its sister funds have no minimum purchase requirement. We mentioned Twentieth Century Cash Reserves in Chapter 7. We have highlighted this fund throughout six editions of this book. As we mentioned earlier, a $100-a-month investment program in Twentieth Century Select Investors since 1981 would be worth over $40,000 today.

The fund's performance has been excellent during the past decade, earning a compounded annual return of 15 percent. The fund was up 40 percent in 1991. *Forbes* rated it "A" (superior) during bull markets and "C" (average) during bear markets.

Twentieth Century Select pays some dividends, but it primarily seeks capital appreciation.

Several other no-load funds have been rated consistently high by *Forbes:*

| Fund | Minimum | Average Annual Return (1980–92) |
|------|---------|---------------------------------|
| Nicholas Fund<br>700 N. Water St.<br>Suite 1010<br>Milwaukee, WI 53202<br>414-272-6133 | $ 500 | 16.0% |
| Lindner Fund<br>P.O. Box 11208<br>St. Louis, MO 63105<br>314-727-5305 | $2,000 | 16.9% |
| Janus Fund<br>100 Fillmore St.<br>Suite 300<br>Denver, CO 80206<br>800-525-3713 | $1,000 | 16.7% |

**Note:** Small investors can get around the minimum requirements for the Janus Fund and the Nicholas Fund (and many other mutual funds) by signing up for an "automatic investment plan." When you fill out a form, these fund organizations will arrange with your bank to have a specified amount transferred automatically each month from your checking account to the fund you select. Both Janus and Nicholas allow you to begin investing with only $50 a month! Call them for more information.

## Families of Funds

Many no-load mutual funds operate as a group and are managed under a single investment account so that you can switch among funds with ease. Many are listed in the newspaper under "Mutual Funds." Some of these include:

The Vanguard Group
P.O. Box 2600
Valley Forge, PA 19482
800-662-7447
215-648-6000

Vanguard funds include: Explorer, Municipal Bond Funds, High-Yield Bond Fund, Windsor Fund, Specialized Funds. Annual expense ratio is usually the lowest in the industry.

Fidelity Group
Devonshire St.
Boston, MA 02109
800-544-8888

Fidelity funds include: Contrafund, Fidelity Fund, Municipal Bond Fund, Magellan Fund, Cash Reserves, Select Portfolios. Most Fidelity funds charge a low load.

T. Rowe Price Group
100 East Pratt St.
Baltimore, MD 21202
800-638-5660

Price funds include: New Income, New Era, New Horizons, Growth Stock, Prime Reserve, International Stock Fund.

The Dreyfus Group
144 Glenn Curtiss Blvd.
Uniondale, NY 11556
800-645-6561

Dreyfus funds include: A Bond Plus, Dreyfus Fund, Third Century Fund, Liquid Assets, Tax-Exempt Bond Funds.

The Scudder Group
160 Federal St.
Boston, MA 02110
800-225-2470

Scudder funds include: International Fund, Japan Fund, Development Fund, Income Fund, Managed Municipal Bonds, Tax-Free Money Fund, Cash Investment Trust.

## Telephone-Switch Privileges

Most mutual fund families offer a telephone-switch service for immediate buying and selling of fund shares. As a shareholder, you can call the toll-free number of the fund and request that shares be transferred to the affiliated money market fund, or vice versa. Thus, you have instant liquidity in the market. Usually, there's no charge for switching, although there may be some restrictions.

The following true story demonstrates how an investor profited by switching within the family of funds in the Vanguard Group.

The customer began with $10,000 at the beginning of the year. He kept his money for the first three and a half months in a money market fund called the Vanguard Money Market Trust, which, at the time, earned him 8 to 9 percent interest on an annualized basis. In March, interest rates started dropping, so he called Vanguard's toll-free number and transferred his money into Vanguard's High-Yield Bond Fund. Within eight weeks, that fund had appreciated 15 percent. In addition, he was earning about 11 percent interest, giving his account a net worth of over $11,500. Finally, foreseeing a rise in the stock market, he switched into Vanguard Windsor Fund, which in the next two months moved up 19 percent! In less than eight months, the customer had turned his $10,000 into $13,600—an annualized gain of approximately 50 percent.

If he had tried to trade the market in individual stocks and bonds, commissions would have cost him $400 to $500, but by using a family fund, he didn't spend a dime on commissions. Even the telephone calls were free!

We often think of millionaires sitting in their master suites making millions in the stock market with just a few phone calls. Well, now the day of the armchair investor has arrived in middle America!

When it comes to telephone-switching among no-load funds, Charles Schwab & Co. provides great flexibility and convenience. Schwab has eliminated the paperwork involved in switching among fund families by bringing together more than 200 funds from various fund families. With a simple toll-free telephone call, you can switch among the 200 funds and pay only a small commission. Jack White & Co., another discount broker, also offers this service.

### Closed-End Funds

There's another kind of mutual fund that is attractive to the small investor: closed-end funds. These are called *closed end* because the number of shares is fixed, or closed, from the beginning. With open-ended funds, the number of shares fluctuates with investor demand for the fund, so the price of the shares is based entirely on the net asset value of the fund. Closed-end funds trade more like stocks on the stock market. Since the number of shares is fixed, the price rises and falls according to investor demand for the fund. If there is a lot of interest in the fund, investors may bid the price up above its underlying stock value. On the other hand, investor apathy regarding a certain fund can cause it to sell at a discount below its net asset value, even though the fund's management may be excellent. These fluctuations provide good buying or selling opportunities.

There are many types of closed-end funds: funds that invest in growth stocks, bonds, government securities, municipal bonds, foreign stocks, and so forth. Most "country funds" are closed-end funds that trade on the New York Stock Exchange (NYSE). They include the Mexico Fund (NYSE: symbol MFX), the Korea Fund (NYSE: KF), the Germany Fund (NYSE: GER), etc. (The Japan Fund is managed by Scudder and is open ended.) Other well-known closed-end funds include the Salomon Brothers Fund (NYSE: SBF), a South African gold fund called ASA (NYSE: ASA), Blue-Chip Value Fund (NYSE: BLU) and the Templeton Emerging Markets Fund (NYSE: EMF).

One of the great advantages for the small investor is that you get excellent money management with an extremely low minimum. Most closed-end funds sell for $10 to $30 a share, so a round lot (100 shares) costs only $1,000 to $3,000. You can even buy fewer than 100 shares if you buy through a discount broker. Suppose you wanted to get in on the booming Third World markets in Asia and Latin America. Selecting individual stocks in these countries would be extremely difficult, but you could invest in Templeton's Emerging Market Fund for only $22 a share (in 1992). That's only $2,200 plus commissions for 100 shares.

Another great advantage of closed-end funds is that they sometimes sell for less than their net asset value, giving investors an opportunity similar to buying stocks at a discount. Sometimes the discount can be as much as 40 percent, as in the case of Convertible Holdings Capital (NYSE: CNV). In 1992, this fund had a net asset value of $11 a share, but was selling for only $7 1/2. Moreover, Convertible Holdings Captial is required to eliminate this discount by 1997. This means that, even if the stock market goes nowhere for the next four to five years, you'll still have a built-in profit of 40 to 50 percent. Another good fund that sells at a significant discount is Quest for Value Capital Fund (NYSE: KFV).

Closed-end funds trade like stocks and must be purchased through a broker. They offer so many advantages that we recommend them regularly in our newsletter, *Forecasts & Strategies*. You may obtain a sample issue by calling 800-777-5005.

## INVESTMENT STRATEGY: SHOULD YOU BUY-AND-HOLD OR TRADE?

Many investors, especially those just starting out, might not feel comfortable with short-term trading. If that's the case, stay with the proven performers, such as Twentieth Century Select Investors, the Nicholas Fund or another top-performing fund, and let their professional managers make your decisions for you. Even then you must be aware that no one can guarantee that future performance will be as good as past performance. Management is prone to change attitudes and trading techniques from year to year. You must be willing to monitor the situation and to switch to another fund or out of stocks entirely if you don't like what you see. What indicators should you be looking for?

Basically, there are two camps in the investment world: the technical chartists and the fundamental analysts. Both camps claim to be right in their forecasts much of the time, and can generally find something important that they overlooked to explain why they went wrong the rest of the time.

No one is right all of the time. But if you understand the markets and have a method or plan for investing, you will have a good chance of winning more often than you lose.

### Is Technical Charting Head and Shoulders above the Rest?

Technical charting is founded on the theory that history repeats itself. Prices of stocks, commodities and even money itself (bonds and interest rates) rise and fall in discernible patterns. Chartists use terms like *head and shoulders, triangles* and *resistance levels* to describe the cycles they observe. By drawing up graphs and charts of these patterns, traders feel that they can predict what the market will do next, and they invest accordingly.

Sounds simple, doesn't it? You just look at the graph, pinpoint exactly where the market is heading and follow the trend. Then place everything you've got to win. With the advent of the computer age, charting has become increasingly sophisticated, utilizing market factors that were often too complicated to include in the past. So why doesn't everyone make a killing every time?

Quite often the chartists are indeed right in their predictions, but no matter how sophisticated the charting may be, there is always the chance that some important factor has been overlooked, and a different pattern will develop instead. When this happens, the chartist simply draws up a new chart.

Our observation has been that a system works for a while and then suddenly stops working. And there is no way of knowing when that will be.

Moreover, the chartist's timing may be slightly off. While a predicted pattern may indeed occur, it might happen in July instead of June, or in 1995 instead of 1996. For the big-time investor who is fully diversified, this is no major crisis, but for the novice investor using everything to buy on margin, a slight mistake in timing can mean disaster.

Remember that no one has a crystal ball, and there is no guaranteed way to make money in the stock market. If it really were a sure thing, there would be millions of buyers—and no one willing to sell.

Nevertheless, if technical trading appeals to you and you wish to avoid those "down" markets from time to time by switching among funds, there are some simple techniques you can use to help your decision making. One service is offered by investment counselor Dick Fabian, who writes the monthly *Telephone Switch Newsletter* (P.O. Box 2538, Huntington Beach, CA 92647; $177 a year). His approach is totally "technical," meaning that he watches the funds' charts rather than their P/E ratio or other market factors to determine whether they are currently a good buy. Over the years, he has been able to profit from the bull markets in the mutual funds and to avoid the bear markets with just a few mistakes. During bull markets, he invests in equity growth funds. During bear markets, he keeps his money safe in money funds. Subscription to the *Telephone Switch Newsletter* includes 12 issues, a 24-hour hotline telephone service and special bulletins, plus a copy of Fabian's book, *How to Be Your Own Investment Counselor—Through the Use of Telephone Switch Mutual Funds.*

## Fundamental Analysis

While many investors are drawn to the exactness of technical trading, others want to know the *whys* behind their stock decisions. They look at changes in the general economy or in a company's performance when making their investment decisions. This trading technique is called "fundamental analysis." Even if you are a technical trader, you should be aware of certain market indicators and monitor their changes.

Here are some of the fundamental indicators you should be watching:

• *The money supply.* This is the amount of money in circulation in the form of cash, checking accounts and savings accounts. The amount of money in circulation is carefully controlled by the Federal Reserve Board.

A modest increase in the money supply that matches the rate of capital growth and expansion may appear beneficial for the economy. But too rapid an increase floods the market, causing inflation and rising prices. On the other hand, "tight money" policy makes cash harder to come by, increasing interest rates as many businesses and individuals compete to borrow fewer dollars. A stable money supply that promotes low inflation and low interest rates is generally good for the economy and signals a good time to be in the stock market.

• *Federal deficits and government spending*. Contrary to political opinion, government spending is not necessarily good for the economy. Since the government produces nothing of its own, it must either borrow or seize (through taxation) all the money it spends. When government borrows, it drives interest rates up, making it more expensive for businesses to acquire investment capital. Or the government "monetizes" the debt by getting the Federal Reserve to print more money, resulting in inflation.

Finally, the government must resort to increasing taxes to confiscatory levels. This can be devastating to the economy, as businesses are forced to cut back in order to pay the tax man. When huge new spending programs are announced, be prepared for rising inflation and lowered prosperity.

• *Interest rates*. Debt isn't always bad. In fact, most businesses rely on a certain amount of debt to increase their profits or to purchase supplies. For example, the owner of a boutique might borrow money to purchase a line of dresses, knowing that in a few months she will have sold enough to pay off the loan and have a nice profit besides. But when interest rates are high, the cost of borrowing money may be prohibitive, and the boutique owner will have to cut back her inventory, reducing her net sales.

High interest rates hurt everyone—business owners who want to expand, consumers who need to borrow for major purchases and future taxpayers who will be liable for government debt.

• *Unemployment*. Unemployment is a fundamental indicator in two ways. Most obviously, people who are out of work are unable to save, unable to buy and often must rely on government handouts to put food on their tables, so unemployment slows the economy down.

It is also an indication of whether business is bad or good, whether companies are cutting back or expanding. This is not a primary market indicator because it tends to lag behind some of the other indicators. But it is useful in determining whether an increase in the stock market is the beginning of a genuine bull market or merely a bear market rally.

• *Political Conditions*. What's happening in Washington, Moscow and the Middle East has a definite effect on the markets in New York and Chicago.

How can you monitor these fundamental market indicators? There are a variety of ways. Subscribing to several good investment advisories is one. Reading the front page and business sections of a good metropolitan newspaper is another. You might want to try charting as well. And nothing teaches like experience—start investing, and see how fast you learn! The important thing is to keep yourself informed, so that when you do make an investment decision, it is your own decision.

## YOUR INVESTMENT PHILOSOPHY

In summary, your investment philosophy is very important when you invest in the stock market. You can be the speculative "hare" by moving in and out of individual stocks or mutual funds for maximum profits. You might even trade in puts and calls, or the financial futures markets, if you dare.

On the other hand, you might be the conservative "tortoise" who carefully selects stocks or mutual funds for maximum appreciation. In fact, many studies have indicated that the selection of a dozen good-quality stocks may well be preferable to trying to beat the market by moving in and out all the time. In the case of mutual funds, the race is ultimately dependent upon the management of the funds, so it's crucial to monitor their performance.

In any case, it's good to know that Wall Street no longer has to be an exotic, faraway land. You can begin investing in the stock market with as little as $50, and you can begin understanding the markets yourself with a trip to the library to read *Value Line Investment Survey* or *Morningstar*. You, too, can own a piece of corporate America.

# CHAPTER 9

# The Lowdown on Real Estate

*Patience in market is worth pounds in a year.*

—Poor Richard's Almanac

$F$OR THE SMALL INVESTOR, real estate can't be beat as an investment opportunity. Here are some advantages:

- You don't need a college education to become a successful investor. Many average citizens have become real estate millionaires.

- You can control large assets with little money of your own. (See the story below about the young man who made $10,000 on his first real estate deal with only $2 in out-of-pocket expenses!)

- You can be heavily in debt, or close to broke, and still buy real estate through *seller financing*.

- You can find incredible below-market bargains in real estate (especially through foreclosures), and sell these properties quickly for huge profits.

- You gain a variety of tax advantages through real estate.

- You have a tangible asset, not just a piece of paper representing ownership in a company.

- Real estate has proven to be a good inflation hedge over the long run.

With all these reasons, you can see why there are so many campaigns on television promoting real estate as the *only way* for the small investor to make money fast. Of course, that isn't true, as we have shown in this book. The small investor can also make it big in stocks, options and other fast-moving investments. In fact, real estate isn't for everyone. Some investors are not comfortable with the large amount of debt inherent in real estate investment. Others don't want to deal with the headaches of landlording, paperwork and the ups and downs of this market. But these are risks many "cash poor" investors are willing to take.

## INCREDIBLE SUCCESS STORIES

Real estate is one of the fastest ways for the "cash poor" investor to build financial independence. Jeff Rickerson, a young man we met on an investment cruise in the Caribbean, is a good example. During the previous year, he had been working as a bank intern in Jefferson City, Missouri. Suddenly he was laid off. He used what little savings he had to attend a seminar on creative real estate. After taking the course, he decided to put what he had learned into practice. One day as he was canvassing a neighborhood, he saw a county worker mowing the lawn at a house.

He could see that the house was furnished, but a little research revealed that it had been unoccupied for nine months. Apparently the owner had skipped town. Jeff contacted the owner by paying $2 at the county courthouse for ownership records and then contacted the post office, which had his forwarding address. The owner had lost his job and moved back to Mississippi. He was still making payments on the house but desperately wanted out.

Jeff offered to take over his mortgage payments and handle all the paperwork by mail so the owner wouldn't have to return. The owner figured that he had some equity in the property, but he just wanted out, so he agreed with the proposal. "He was really grateful," Jeff told us.

Jeff found a partner who could co-sign the deal. That way he could qualify for taking over the mortgage payments at the bank. The mortgage balance was $43,000. He and the partner agreed to split the profits from the house when it sold.

Before Jeff finalized the purchase of the house, he had already advertised to sell it. He and his partner arranged to have the property fixed up, but they didn't pay anyone until the closing. Jeff found someone willing to buy the house for $69,000, the market price.

The closings for both the purchase and the sale of the house took place on the same day. Jeff used a little over $2 out of his own pocket. After closing costs, he made $10,000 on the deal—and proceeded to attend another conference on creative real estate, this one taking place on a well-deserved Caribbean cruise.

Granted, the story of Jeff Rickerson is unusual, but we have met hundreds of people like him who have made big money on little deals in real estate.

One highly successful woman told us that she originally started buying real estate because she hated paying higher and higher taxes every year. Her goal was to buy enough property to offset her husband's income, thereby reducing their tax liability to zero. And she did it. She confided, however, that her husband never did fully understand how she did it, so when they divorced a few years later, she gladly let him keep the cars and the bank account while she retained ownership of the rental properties. She chuckled, "Today he's still slaving at his job and paying a fortune in taxes, while I work at my leisure, buying a good property when it comes along and living off the rental income in the meantime. Best of all, I still manage to pay very little taxes."

There are numerous other examples of investors with very little in savings who have profited from real estate. While we were in college renting rooms in the dorms, we had a friend who bought a small older house near campus. It was run down but in a good location for students. He put $500 down, moved into one of the rooms himself and rented the others to students. Their rent covered his mortgage payments, so he had free student housing for himself. He spent his spare time fixing the place up, and when he sold the house a few years later, he pocketed a profit of nearly $20,000, which he used to buy two more houses. He also gained valuable business knowledge from the experience. Now this friend has a sizeable portfolio—because he wasn't willing to "throw his money away" in rent.

Another friend of ours did the same thing, buying and selling several properties while going to college. He eventually turned his experience into a book, a seminar program and a full-time business. This real estate entrepreneur? Robert Allen of *No Money Down* fame.

## JOHN SCHAUB'S 10-10-10 FORMULA

Keep in mind that no investment can remain on top forever, and the smart investor needs to be flexible when choosing investments. While real estate does still provide many outstanding investment opportunities, the prudent investor needs to be much more selective today than 10 years ago.

We have always liked investment adviser John Schaub's conservative approach to real estate investing, which he calls "big money on little deals." He calls it the "10-10-10" plan: Look for a home in a good neighborhood that is 10 percent below comparable market prices, put no more than 10 percent down and pay no more than 10 percent interest. In the past, such deals have not been easy to find, but with the huge number of foreclosures going on these days, it may now be easier than you think. Schaub is extremely selective—he aims to buy just one good house a year. He says his best deals come from people who have lived in their homes for a long time, have a large equity and are willing to help you with the financing.

After seven years and seven houses, he sells the first house and replaces it, so he gets maximum depreciation, good rental income and is not overwhelmed by managing too many houses. His method works regardless of economic conditions because it relies on consumer demand, not inflation, to turn a profit. For detailed information on his method, contact John Schaub, 1938 Ringling Blvd., Sarasota, FL 34236, 800-237-9222. He offers a cassette-tape series and workbook entitled "Big Money on Little Deals" for $149. We highly recommend it if you are serious about real estate.

## WHAT KIND OF REAL ESTATE SHOULD YOU BUY?

Where should you look for the best investment real estate? Commercial real estate is the most risky. Bargains are available in many major cities where overbuilding has taken place, but even at a bargain price, commercial property may be hard to lease.

We recommend single-family homes in good neighborhoods where you will easily attract good-quality renters. Vacancy is one of the largest and most frustrating costs a landlord faces. Consequently, you want to choose rental properties that will attract long-term tenants. Single-family homes are also the most liquid and most stable in price, compared to commercial properties, apartment complexes, townhouses and duplexes.

If a single-family home is beyond your financial reach at this point, you might consider as a second choice a townhouse, condominium or duplex. These usually sell for considerably less than detached homes and can rent for nearly as much (although they often are harder to sell). Before you buy, investigate other rentals in the development. How do they compare to the unit you are considering? How much do they rent for? What is the current vacancy rate, and how rapid is the turnover? Is there a steady source of tenants from a military base, university, elected government or other transient community? What are the condo fees?

In most cases, you should avoid brand-new developments that promise to be worth double or triple the selling price in 10 years but have no actual track record. The developer may be sincere in his prediction that the city is growing in this direction and that this will be the hot neighborhood of the next decade, but his sincerity does not necessarily make him right. All too often, a developer's high hopes turn into dashed dreams, and he is forced to sell his last few units at greatly reduced rates. That is your real opportunity to buy.

## FORECLOSURES: THE GROWTH INDUSTRY OF THE 1990s!

Today the best bargains in real estate can be found in foreclosures. Foreclosed properties are available from homeowners, developers, banks, insurance companies and government agencies. Every recession causes financial trouble and bankruptcies for homeowners and businesses. Thousands of properties are foreclosed on by the underlying mortgage company, which attempts to sell the foreclosed property either individually or by auction. With the ongoing bank crisis and intermittent recessions, foreclosures are on the rise.

Where can you find foreclosures? Banks are required to give public notice of their intent to foreclose several weeks before the auction is to take place, so you can find potential foreclosures among the legal notices in the newspaper.

Another source of information on potential foreclosures is an attorney who specializes in them. If you can get on friendly terms with an attorney who handles delinquent mortgages and let it be known that you have money available for such investments, you could find a few good deals.

Another excellent source is a good, innovative real estate agent. Real estate agents are often the first to know about a potential foreclosure. Establish a good rapport with several agents. Let them know that you have the money for quick sales as long as the price—and the commission—are favorable. Always start out with a very low offer. When the homeowners are in no position to offer special financing and when time is crucial to avoid foreclosure, they are likely to accept.

Finally, the federal government has frequent auctions of foreclosed properties. The Resolution Trust Corporation, the IRS, the Department of Veterans Affairs, Ginnie Mae and Fannie Mae also offer auctions from time to time at bargain prices.

## BUYING A FORECLOSURE *BEFORE* AN AUCTION

Sometimes you can make a lot of money by buying a home on which the owner has defaulted but the house has not yet been foreclosed. An investor can expect to save 15 to 20 percent on a home that has a five- or six-year-old mortgage, and save even more on an older home. This is possible because you simply take over the mortgage and begin making back payments. Your reward is getting the equity in the home. Let a few real estate brokers know that you would be interested in making an offer on such a deal. And then drive a hard bargain.

No one buys a house with the intention of falling behind in payments, but adverse circumstances can arise, and when they do, the owner is faced with the prospect of losing his credit rating as well as his house. This potential loss is your trump card as an investor.

Some real estate experts recommend looking for foreclosure deals wherein the house is already vacant, indicating that the owner has already accepted the inevitable. Track the owner down, explain what is going to happen by such-and-such a date, remind him of his credit rating and then present your offer to take the house and its burdens off his hands.

Picking up foreclosures is not as simple as a typical real estate deal. You must be very careful of the legal obligations that may come with your assumption of the deed. Before filing the owner's quit-claim deed and accepting full responsibility for the property, you should have a thorough title search conducted. There may be liens against the property for which you would otherwise become responsible.

You should also check for "due on sale" clauses in the mortgage, which may impose prepayment penalties, raise the interest rate or require that the loan be paid off immediately when the title is transferred to a new owner. Beware of any clause that limits your freedom to resell the property. Even if your title search is satisfactory, you should purchase title insurance—just in case. You might even make your bid conditional upon your ability to obtain title insurance (although if it is a hot property with several interested buyers, your contingency may be rejected).

Each state has its own rules about foreclosures, and you should become familiar with your state's laws.

In summary, purchasing a potential foreclosure can be a good way to profit in the real estate market, as long as you do it right. With pre-foreclosures, deal directly with the owner, preferably one who has already vacated the house. Examine the house carefully and have its value appraised, both for resale and for rental. Conduct a thorough title search, and purchase title insurance. Although time is of the essence, be cautious. Fools rush in where seasoned investors fear to tread. Remember these five rules:

1. Never buy a property without looking at it. If it is impossible to get inside before the sale, at least look through windows or check the architectural plans at the courthouse.

2. Never buy a house without knowledge of comparable values.

3. Before the auction, establish a maximum bid based on your minimum profit spread.

4. Never buy in a slum or deteriorating area. Look for distressed sellers, not distressed property.

5. Secure a thorough title report, checking the status of all outstanding liens and any state regulations.

## Buying at Auction

Real estate auctions occur frequently in all major cities in the United States. They are conducted by banks, developers, the IRS, the Department of Veterans Affairs, the Resolution Trust Corporation (RTC), Ginnie Mae and other government agencies. They are usually advertised in the classifieds of the local newspaper. If you decide to buy at auction, call ahead so you understand the exact procedure and the time and location. Ask whether the bidder must have cash-in-full on the spot. It is a good idea to attend a few auctions before bidding.

## Cash Is King!

Remember that cash is king at auctions. Investors who can pay cash for a property are more likely to get a foreclosure at auction than someone who has to finance. One of the students in our investment class at Rollins College recently bought a three-bedroom house at a VA auction. Several offers were made above his $40,000 bid, but he got the house because he was willing to pay cash. Then, after he bought the house, he took out a $30,000 mortgage. Even with the mortgage, he's getting positive cash flow on his investment.

## OTHER OPPORTUNITIES FOR REAL ESTATE BARGAINS

While foreclosures offer the best bargains today in real estate, there may be other unique opportunities. Experts suggest you look for homeowners having to relocate, homeowners getting a divorce and people needing to get out of their real estate as soon as possible.

## Relocations

Quite often, when an employee is being transferred to a different office in another part of the country, the employer will ease the burden of moving by promising to buy the employee's house if it hasn't sold within three to six months. Later, the company may be willing to sell the property for less than it paid, just to get rid of the liability. We once saved $40,000 on the purchase of a relocation deal, simply because the company didn't want to be bothered with marketing the house, and we were willing to settle fast.

## Divorce Sales

Gone are the days when a husband got his walking papers and the wife got everything else. Now divorce agreements tend to divide property equally, and that usually means selling the house. In these sales, price is often secondary to speed of sale. If you have ready cash for a good-sized down payment and a good credit rating for a speedy mortgage, you can often purchase a nice home in a fine neighborhood for 10 to 15 percent under the market price.

## CREATIVE FINANCING

When you buy a house or a rental property, what kind of financing should you use? In some cases, choosing the right mortgage has become more complicated than choosing the right house. Should you take a fixed-rate mortgage for 15 years, an adjustable-rate mortgage for 30 years or something in between? Moreover, you must consider the cost of *points,* the one-time loan origination fee paid at closing which equals a percentage of the loan amount. One point equals one percent. Charging points is the bank's way of hiding a higher interest rate and getting around any state usury laws that may limit the amount they are allowed to charge. One lender might be offering a 9 percent loan with 1.5 points, while another will charge only 8 percent if you pay 3.5 points. A third company might offer 8.5 percent with only 1.5 points but at an adjustable rate. In this case, the mortgage could rise as much as five points (or it could fall), depending on the Treasury-bill rate. Check with your lender to find the best financing for your situation.

To determine the best loan for your house, you must consider two things. First, how long do you plan to keep the house? And second, what direction do you think interest rates are going? If you plan to keep the house for several years, take the loan with the lower fixed interest rate and pay the higher points. This is because, over the long run, the high initial costs will be recaptured by the lower payments.

If, on the other hand, you consider this a rental that you plan to resell quickly, then it would be better to reduce your points and pay the higher interest rate for the two or three years. Incidentally, if you do anticipate selling the house in fewer than five years, make sure there is no prepayment penalty, which could cost you an additional two points or so when you close out the loan.

## What about Adjustable-Rate Mortgages?

Adjustable-rate mortgages certainly are tempting these days. Interest rates for adjustable-rate mortgages (ARMs) are always lower than fixed rates, and this could make a sizeable difference in your monthly payments. Most ARM loans have an interest cap, both annually and over the lifetime of the loan. For example, most ARMs are tied to the Treasury-bill rate and are adjusted once a year. A typical loan would have a cap of 2 percent per year, meaning that even if T-bills increased by 10 percent, your mortgage rate would increase only by 2 percent each year until it reached a maximum total increase of 5 percentage points. At that point, even if T-bills climbed to 20 percent or more, your mortgage would not increase.

Obviously, with an ARM, you are at the mercy of the economy.

Even with the rate cap, your monthly payment could increase by more than 50 percent. Many people could end up losing their houses. It's a risk you must consider carefully, especially if you expect to keep the house for more than three or four years.

If you do choose an ARM, read the fine print carefully. Some limit the amount that your payment can increase, while placing no annual cap on your actual mortgage rate. If interest rates suddenly skyrocket, your payments will increase only nominally. But the true interest rate will be nibbling away at your equity. This is called *negative amortization*, but *gobbling* might be a better description.

Finally, consider shorter-term mortgages—those that mature in 15 or 20 years rather than the usual 30. You can save tens of thousands of dollars over the course of the mortgage.

If you already have a 30-year mortgage, you can still reduce your total mortgage cost through accelerated payments. By making an additional payment each year and applying it toward the principal, you can reduce the life of your loan by one-third or more. Contact your mortgage company for details.

## Owner Financing

Owner financing at below market rates may offer a lot more advantages than dealing directly with a bank or mortgage company. In some cases, the owners may be willing to finance all or part of your loan themselves. They may be in a hurry to sell, and you may be their only prospect. Or perhaps they are retiring and would rather have steady monthly income than a lump sum. Not many sellers are willing or able to finance the whole house, but many will take back a second mortgage for the difference between what the bank will lend you and the selling price. Make financing a part of your offer. If the sellers are adamant about the asking price, give it to them—but insist on a lower interest rate on the owner-financed mortgage.

Owner financing keeps things a lot simpler, and terms are often more to your advantage. Another advantage is that you don't have to produce your tax returns as you do when you go through the bank or mortgage company in order to qualify for the loan.

## Warning about Creative Finance

A word of caution is in order, about the "creative" approach to real estate: It can get you into trouble. Buying real estate with "no money down" or buying real estate with "more than 100 percent financing" (where you end up with money in your pocket) can spell trouble down the road. Sometimes the speculative artist can play the real estate game as long as he can pay the interest, while she counts on inflation to bring him through in the end. This approach works best during times of high inflation, when the economy helps to boost your investment. But you can't always count on inflation, except to raise your costs!

## EXAMINE ALL THE COSTS

Real estate is not like other investments. You can put your gold coins, stock certificates, bank statements and cold cash into a safe-deposit box and ignore them, but rental properties require a lot of work and attention. Before becoming a landlord, you need to examine all the costs, both of time and money.

First, let's discuss money. It's easy to determine your mortgage and tax expenditures, and then compare the cost to your expected rents. If the rent is higher than the mortgage, you're in business, right?

Too many first-time landlords end up in foreclosure because of this kind of thinking, overlooking the numerous hidden costs. Consider maintenance, for example. Houses are always breaking down and wearing out, and the landlord is responsible for their upkeep. For the landlord on a low budget, this can present a serious problem. You should put part of your rental income into a special fund, to be used for such major expenses as replacing the hot-water heater, roof or aluminum siding.

You can avoid the hassle and expense of minor repairs by including a clause in rental contracts stipulating that the tenant is responsible for the first $50 of all repairs. This will benefit you in two ways. First, you will not be bothered every time a faucet leaks or the dishwasher fails to come on. Second, you will attract the kind of tenant who is a do-it-yourselfer, and will not expect you, as landlord, to fix everything.

Also consider the cost of vacancy. Frequent vacancies can destroy your real estate profits. Not only will you lose potential income, but you will need to spend additional money between tenants making cosmetic repairs. Consequently, you need to find tenants who will be likely to stay. When advertising your property, establish a rental price that is slightly under the market price for that neighborhood. This will encourage numerous callers and will give you the opportunity to choose the best tenants. Sometimes a longer lease is more profitable than a higher rent.

Another way to increase rental income is to rent by the room or even the bed, rather than renting the whole house or apartment. For example, if you owned an apartment building or fourplex near a university, you might be able to rent it for a mere $250 to a student couple or family. But that same two-bedroom apartment could be rented to individual students, two to a room, for $125 each, thus doubling your income. Admittedly, the wear and tear from individual students would probably be greater than that from a family, but a sizeable security deposit and the increased income may protect you from major damage.

A common mistake made by first-time landlords is that of treating their tenants like friends or family. Or worse, renting to actual friends or family! Business is business, and you will be a more successful real estate entrepreneur if you always use a standard rental contract for all your tenants, including security deposit and payment of the last month's rent, if that is standard in your area. Have all utilities charged to the name of the tenants, even if it means they will have to pay an additional security deposit to the utility company. Don't let your heart rule your pocketbook, or they might both wind up empty.

## INVESTING FOR A QUICK TURNAROUND

If "landlording" isn't for you, you may be more interested in the "buy low, sell high" approach to real estate. Many people have made small fortunes by purchasing old homes, fixing them up and reselling them in less than a year. Often couples will restore one home at a time, living in the house while they are fixing it up. This is actually more occupation than investment, because it requires more than money! Still, if you enjoy carpentry, landscaping and decorating, this could be an enjoyable way to profit.

Follow these simple steps, which can help you select the right property and prepare it for renting or resale:

*Step 1.* Buy a small residential property that is undervalued. "Small residential property" means a single-family home, condominium, townhouse, duplex or fourplex. Commercial property, such as an office building, may seem appealing because it can provide "cash flow" (where your rent revenue is greater than your mortgage and operating costs), but during a recession, when offices are hard to rent, you can be stuck with a heavy mortgage and not enough money to meet the payments. Residential property is far more stable and suitable for the small investor.

"Undervalued property" means a house that is located in a good area but that is run down or in need of repair. You can buy it at a distressed price because most prospective buyers are turned off by the appearance of the house. It may need paint, a new driveway, work on the lawn, more modern kitchen appliances, new carpet or a host of other cosmetic improvements. It is absolutely imperative, however, that this kind of house be located in a decent neighborhood. Remember that you're searching for the small, substandard home in an otherwise standard neighborhood. Unless you want to be a slumlord, don't buy a run-down home in a neighborhood full of run-down homes.

*Step 2.* Make cosmetic improvements that don't cost a great deal. Look for property that has a solid foundation, something that would be quite desirable if it were fixed up. Then make repairs that will increase the value of the property by several times the cost of the improvements. Real estate experts agree that the following cosmetic changes can add a great deal to the resale value of real estate:

- Paint and wallpaper

- Simple landscaping

- Cleanup (grounds, basement, interior)

- Replacement of outdated fixtures

- Replacement of carpet

- New kitchen and bathroom fixtures, floors, etc.

- New or refurbished front door

These items will usually add more value to your property than they cost.

Real estate experts consider the kitchen and the bathroom to be the most important rooms when showing a house or apartment. Improvements in these areas will prove to be the most profitable when seeking a quick resale. Just having them sparkling clean and fingerprint-free can be a vast improvement.

There are certain improvements that generally will not increase the value of the home significantly and that you should therefore avoid. These include adding a swimming pool, a garage, storm windows, luxury appliances (such as a trash compactor), a new roof, a finished basement or a barbecue.

*Step 3.* Sell the residential property without a real estate agent for maximum profit. When you sell your property, use the profits to make larger purchases. Even if real estate prices are "soft" at the time you sell, your cosmetic improvements can bring you substantial profits. Use these profits to purchase more under-valued homes in your area.

The *residential property fix-up* approach is the safest, soundest way to build a small fortune in real estate. It is the approach that Bill Nickerson used to become a multimillionaire. If home renovation appeals to you, you should read Bill Nickerson's classic book, *How I Turned $1,000 into Three Million in Real Estate—in My Spare Time!* (Simon & Schuster). This is capitalism at its best, enhancing the beauty of the community while still providing a handsome profit for the entrepreneur. Who needs government reclamation projects and subsidized housing when there's a free-market capitalist around?

## HOW TO REDUCE THE COST OF BUYING AND SELLING

Once you've worked hard at finding the right house, negotiated the best deal, fixed the house up, rented it, maintained it and finally decided to sell it, you'll want to keep as much of the profit for yourself as possible. A full-time real estate agent can provide you with excellent service and benefits, but you will pay 5 to 7 percent of the selling price for the convenience. As an investor, you will probably want to eliminate the middle person and sell the house through less expensive methods.

The least expensive but most time-consuming method is called *for sale by owner,* or FSBO (pronounced "fizbo"). If you sell the house yourself, you retain all the profit. Advertise frequently in the weekend paper, and use a catchy opening phrase to attract the scanner's attention. Keep a sign prominently displayed and, if your house is located near a side street, have one near the major road as well. Don't overlook advertising in small community newspapers and bulletin boards. If the house is in a good neighborhood or in a desirable location for commuters, as we have recommended, you should be able to sell in a fairly short time. Expect to hear from other real estate investors, like yourself, who are looking for a good house in a good neighborhood at a bargain price. But if you have fixed the house up nicely for resale, you should be able to demand and receive a full market price.

You may want to rent your house temporarily while waiting to find the right buyer. Homes are more appealing to potential buyers when they aren't empty, and the extra income will offset your mortgage costs. Moreover, you may find a buyer in your rental by using a lease option agreement.

One way to ensure that tenants will take good care of your house and remain for several years is to let them rent with an option to buy. You can increase the rent by $100 to $200, setting aside that amount toward their eventual down payment when they exercise the option. This amounts to a forced savings program for the tenant who needs a down payment. Meanwhile, you have an interest-free loan. If the tenant decides to exercise the option, you have a buyer without paying any further advertising costs or real estate commissions!

## THE TAX ADVANTAGES OF REAL ESTATE

One of the biggest advantages of real estate investing has always been the tax angle. Prior to the 1986 tax act, Americans could buy real estate and write off practically everything against their regular income. They could write off the interest, real estate taxes, insurance and, most important, the value of the property through liberal depreciation rules.

But in 1986, Congress changed the rules regarding deductions allowed for real estate, making it virtually impossible for the part-time investor to offset real estate losses against ordinary income. Nevertheless, it is still possible for the conservative investor to *reduce* tax burdens through real estate. You can still take advantage of deductions for interest, taxes, insurance, the cost of repairs and depreciation.

Suppose you buy a $110,000 duplex with $10,000 down and finance the remaining $100,000 at 10 percent. Your monthly payment (principal, interest, taxes and insurance) will be approximately $1,000, depending on your local tax structure. You will be able to deduct all interest payments (approximately $10,000 the first year), all taxes (probably $500 to $1,500) and, on investment property, all insurance premiums.

If you fix a leaky toilet, patch a roof or replace a broken rail for a tenant, the cost is tax deductible. There is a distinction between "repairs" and "improvements," however. For tax purposes, repairs are changes that bring a property back to its original condition, while improvements make the property worth more than it was before. Thus, replacing a broken dishwasher hose is a repair, while remodeling the kitchen is an improvement. The former will merit you a $50 deduction; the latter will have to be depreciated, and the tax benefit spread over several years. Generally, if the change is expected to last for more than a year or if it costs more than about $200, the IRS will probably consider it an improvement.

Depreciation is the main tax attraction of real estate. It allows you eventually to deduct the entire cost of your investment property. The theory behind depreciation is that your tangible asset has a physical life span and that it will eventually become worthless by either breaking down or wearing out. The tax code allows you to stretch that eventual loss over the entire life of the asset. Different assets have different life expectancies and, therefore, different depreciation tables. Currently commercial real estate (including rental homes) can be depreciated over 27.5 years.

Congress has consistently chipped away at real estate deductions over the past decade, and you never know when the rules will change again. For instance, the sweeping tax reform of 1986 made it impossible for the real estate tycoon to "zero out" his taxes anymore. For that reason, we recommend that you maintain a conservative real estate portfolio. Purchase single-family homes that are in prime locations at prices that will not saddle you with negative cash flow. And don't rely on tax advantages to give you profit. Most important, diversify. Don't let real estate be your only investment.

## REAL ESTATE: THE FINAL WORD

Real estate belongs in the well-diversified portfolio. Your personal residence may be your only investment in this field, or you may want to branch out into some of the more speculative areas of real estate investments mentioned in this chapter.

# CHAPTER 10

# Where To Earn High Monthly Income

*He who is rich need not live sparingly, and he who can live sparingly need not be rich.*

—Poor Richard's Almanac

It is an obvious fact, but it bears repeating: Different investors have different financial goals. The investment needs of a couple in their thirties with three young children and little or no savings or equity will vary greatly from those of a retired widow with a paid-off mortgage and a Social Security check. The young couple is looking for long-term accumulation of wealth, possibly to save for a home, college education, or orthodontia for their children. On the other hand, the widow needs money for *today*, not 20 years from now.

This chapter is devoted to the needs of retirees, widows and others on "fixed" incomes who need a supplemental income for daily living expenses that will keep up with inflation.

There are several traditional sources of regular investment income, as well as some sources you may not have considered before. In this chapter, we'll recommend low-minimum, low-commission sources of monthly income.

## LOW-RISK INCOME SOURCES

Let's start with the low-risk investments: money market funds, money market accounts and bank CDs. We discussed these low-risk choices in Chapter 7. With bank investments, up to $100,000 of the value of your principal is guaranteed. Interest varies daily on money funds and accounts. The yield on CDs varies with the length of maturity: A five-year CD will pay more than a six-month certificate. But the price of that higher yield is liquidity: If you want to withdraw your money early, you will pay a penalty that will significantly reduce your effective yield. Only you can decide how long you want to tie up your money.

Money funds and CDs have been paying such low interest rates recently that income seekers are looking elsewhere for high income. Let's look at the best alternatives.

## HIGH-YIELDING BONDS

Many conservative investors prefer bonds over stocks because they are less risky. Unlike a stock, a bond does not represent ownership in a company but is a loan made to the company. The price of a stock will fluctuate, but the face value and interest payments of a bond remain constant. Typically, the interest rate on a long-term bond, one that matures in 15 to 30 years, is considerably higher than that on bank CDs or money funds.

There are several risks to bonds: The face value may stay the same, but if you have to sell before the bond matures, you may get less than the face value if interest rates have gone up since you bought. There is also the risk of default—if the underlying company is unable to pay you the principal and interest. You should always be aware of the safety rating of the bond you are buying.

There are numerous types of bonds, each with features that will appeal to different investors. Let's look at a few.

• *Corporate bonds* are issued by the same companies that issue publicly traded stock. Like stocks themselves, the safety and yield of corporate bonds vary according to the safety and profitability of the company. The riskier the bond, the higher the interest rate. You might be able to find a bond yielding a tempting 15 to 16 percent, but if the company is facing bankruptcy, you could lose your principal before the bond matures. You want high income, but you need protection as well. Fortunately, there are two rating services that help you determine the safety of a corporate bond. Standard & Poor's and Moody's both give reliable evaluations. For safety, stay with bonds that are rated between AAA and BBB or between Aaa and Bbb by reliable rating agencies.

Corporate bonds rated below BBB are considered less than "investment grade," and are often referred to as "junk bonds." Junk bonds typically pay 3 to 4 percentage points more than high-quality corporate issues, so you are compensated for taking a higher risk. Be aware, however, that these higher yield bonds are much more volatile. During a recession, they can lose half their value, and during an economic recovery, they can rise rapidly in price. Junk bonds are not for the faint-hearted, but high-income seekers may wish to consider them as a high-risk alternative.

Purchasing a bond on the primary market is very straightforward. You agree to loan the issuing company a certain amount of money (usually at least $1,000) for a certain number of years (usually 15 years or longer) at a specified fixed interest rate. You collect interest payments every six months, and when the bond matures you get your entire principal back. You know right from the outset exactly what to expect. Over 80 percent of bond owners hold their bonds to maturity.

While bonds do have a predetermined face value that will be paid at maturity, the interim price of a bond can fluctuate widely over its lifetime. The reason for this is simple, although the formula for determining a fair price may be more complicated. It is based on fluctuating interest rates.

For example, suppose you wanted to sell a bond with a yield of

8 percent, but prevailing interest rates on newly issued bonds have risen to 12 percent. Because the interest rate on your bond (known as the "coupon rate") is unchangeable, you would have to reduce your selling price so the effective yield would equal a market rate. In short, the price of your bond declines.

A basic rule to remember is that bond prices rise when interest rates are dropping and fall when interest rates are rising.

• *Convertible bonds* are offered by many growth companies. These give you the guaranteed return of a bond, or loan, with the growth potential of a stock, or share in the company. Investors purchase the bond with a guaranteed rate of return, but they have the option of converting it to stock at a predetermined price. That conversion price is usually considerably higher than the current price, so the stock would have to appreciate quite a bit before the investor would exercise the option. The best convertibles are the few that are priced close to the underlying stock price—IBM's convertible bond is a good example. This added profit potential comes at a cost, of course; interest on convertibles is always lower than on regular bonds. Still, convertibles can be a good way to test a company before buying its stock.

• *Municipal bonds* (or "munis") were once the mainstay of every retirement portfolio. They provided regular monthly income and, because they were exempt from federal taxation and were unregistered, they were relatively private. Most munis are still exempt from federal taxation, but new ones are registered with your Social Security number when you buy them, and you are supposed to report income from them. To avoid state reporting requirements, you should invest in double-tax-free bonds, which are free from both federal tax and state tax in the state of issue.

Munis are issued by local governments to finance such projects as parks, schools, civic centers and airports. Apart from the risk of rising inflation and interest rates, your biggest risk is that the municipality might declare bankruptcy before your bond comes due. You can guard against this by investigating the fiscal policy of the municipality, checking the rating given to the bond by a reliable rating agency or by investing in a municipal bond fund, which would spread the risk among many different munis.

## TREASURY SECURITIES

Treasury bills, notes and bonds are considered by many as the safest and the most conservative investments you can make. They pay a guaranteed rate of return and are backed by the federal government. However, that does not make them a good long-term investment. During the inflationary 1970s, they were a very poor investment, as double-digit inflation wiped out the purchasing power of the meager 6 to 7 percent rate of return. In the 1980s, however, during a time of deregulation and falling interest rates, Treasuries made a comeback. Over the long run, Treasuries, like most other bonds, are subject to losses from inflation and taxation.

There are three kinds of Treasury investments: bills, notes and bonds. The main difference among them is the length of time to maturity. Bills are short-term investments (a year or less), notes are medium-term (2 to 10 years) and bonds are long-term debt obligations (10 to 25 years).

• *Treasury bills* mature in 90 days, 182 days or one year. They are sold at a discount from their par (face) value, and the difference between the amount you pay and the amount you receive at maturity reflects the interest yield. Interest rates on new bills fluctuate weekly and are determined at auction; investors from all over the country bid various rates, and those who bid at or under the average rate "win" the opportunity to buy the T-bills that week. Minimum face-value is $10,000, putting T-bills out of reach for the average investor. Consequently, many people invest indirectly through money market funds.

• *Treasury bonds* are typically issued with a minimum face value of $1,000, and mature in 10 to 35 years. They carry a fixed interest rate that is paid semiannually.

• *Treasury notes* are similar to bonds except they have a shorter maturity date, from 2 to 10 years. They come in denominations of $1,000 and interest is paid semiannually.

One of the most attractive features of Treasury securities is their liquidity. There is an active secondary market, so you can sell your bonds quickly if you need the cash. Unlike CDs and money market funds, they are exempt from state and local taxes, so if you live in a state that imposes a high income tax, they are even more desirable.

Treasury securities are offered for sale through branches of the Federal Reserve Bank. You can also buy them through a commercial bank or securities dealer, but you will pay a small commission.

While Treasury securities are considered safe investments for now, many people won't touch them. They are opposed to investing in Treasury securities for the same reason that they wouldn't loan money to friends or relatives who are already deeply in debt. They don't loan money to the federal government because they know that one more debt is the last thing our grandchildren need. Contrary to the enthusiastic advertising, there is nothing patriotic about "buying bonds." When the government needs more money, it creates it out of thin air by printing up securities and selling them to investors. The government has no real product to sell, and you are actually buying nothing but a piece of the national debt. With its power to create money, the Federal Reserve expands the money supply and causes inflation. Yes, you will always get the face value of your T-bills back, but it is possible that by the time you do, inflation will have reduced their purchasing power.

On the other hand, we realize that many Americans must rely on safety and high yield to make ends meet, so we are not critical of those who buy Treasuries, and are comfortable with including information about them in this book.

### Series EE Bonds

The minimum investment for a Treasury bond is $1,000. To encourage everyone to invest in government securities, Congress created a special low-cost bond, called the Series E bond, with a face value of $25 and a discounted price of about $18. After seven years of compounding at a fixed 6 percent rate, your $18 would grow to $25.

The old Series E bond is no longer available, but a new one has taken its place—the *Series EE bond*, with a competitive interest rate and a low minimum that make it attractive to the average investor. Rather than the fixed rate of return that killed the single E bond, these new Series EE bonds have a fluctuating rate that is 85 percent of the Treasury note rate. When compounding is taken into account, the rate actually turns out to be 2 to 3 percent higher than typical bank rates.

There are several advantages to investing in the new Series EE bonds:

- These bonds start with denominations as low as $50 and increase in value up to $10,000. They are sold at a discount, currently one-half their face value.

- Savings bonds can be purchased from any issuing agent, and most banks are issuing agents. Many large companies have payroll deduction plans that invest in U.S. savings bonds.

- Instead of the low fixed-rate interest that made the old Series E bonds a losing investment during the inflationary 1970s, these new Series EE bonds fluctuate with the prevailing Treasury rates. If the T-note rate rises to 10 percent, for example, you will earn 85 percent of that, or about 8.5 percent.

- Your principal is backed by the "full faith and credit" of the U.S. government. Although interest fluctuates with the Treasury note rate, there is a guaranteed minimum return of 6 percent, so that even when interest rates fall below 8 percent, your return will remain at least 6 percent. You are also protected against loss, fire or theft because the bond is recorded in your name and will be replaced if something happens to your certificate.

- Series EE bonds are exempt from state income tax, and federal income tax is deferred until you actually sell the bond. Consequently, you can reinvest all interest earnings, rather than just the after-tax profits, thus increasing your yield.

There is a significant disadvantage to investing in savings bonds, however. There is an early withdrawal penalty that requires you to hold the bond at least five years to earn the full yield. If you sell the bond sooner, your return is significantly reduced. If you hold it only six months, for example, you will receive only a 4 percent annualized return. After one year, the yield on early withdrawals increases to 5.5 percent, and it will increase by about 0.25 percent per year after that. Obviously, these savings bonds require a long-term commitment.

For further information, contact the bond officer at your local bank, or write for a free pamphlet about Series EE bonds to the Bureau of Public Debt, Parkersburg, WV 26106, 304-420-6112.

## THE ADVANTAGE OF BOND FUNDS

If you purchase bonds individually through a broker, you'll have to invest the full minimum of $1,000, $5,000 or even $25,000 for individual bonds, and you'll be charged a commission. A less expensive and more convenient plan is to invest in a no-load fund that carries bonds, preferred stocks and other income-oriented investments. You can choose funds that specialize in a particular kind of bond, while investing as little as $500.

If you are investing for long-term appreciation, you will want to have all dividends reinvested automatically in order to increase your number of shares. But if you are seeking monthly income, you can choose to have dividends paid to you on a regular basis instead.

Here are some good "high grade" bond funds:

| Fund | Recent Yield |
|------|-------------:|
| Dreyfus A Bonds Plus<br>144 Glenn Curtiss Blvd.<br>Uniondale, NY 11556<br>800-645-6561 | 8.4% |
| Investment Grade Income Fund<br>P.O. Box 2600<br>Valley Forge, PA 19482<br>800-662-7447<br>215-648-6000 | 8.9% |
| Scudder Income Fund<br>160 Federal St.<br>Boston, MA 02110<br>800-225-2470 | 8.2% |

One of the major drawbacks to bonds is that your principal can lose value if interest rates go up. This is also true of bond *funds*, but at least with bond funds, you can conveniently switch out of the fund at any time without penalty and put your money into something else, such as a money market fund, a stock fund or a gold fund. Owning shares in a fund gives you greater liquidity and flexibility than owning an individual bond. Bond funds also allow you to diversify into a wide variety of bonds.

## HIGH-YIELD INCOME FUNDS
## (OPEN END AND CLOSED END)

You can earn even higher monthly income by investing in *high-yield income funds*. These funds usually contain bonds that are considered more risky for U.S. investors, either lower-grade corporate bonds (so-called "junk" bonds) or foreign bonds.

Most high-yielding bond funds are "load" funds, but one no-load with a good track record is Vanguard Fixed Income—High

Yield (see address below). Its yield was recently around 10 percent.

Another alternative is *closed-end bond funds*, mutual funds that trade on the stock exchanges. They pay dividends monthly. Most closed-end bond funds sell above their net asset value, but occasionally you may find a closed-end bond fund that trades at a discount. These are the best buys. Closed-end bond funds, including their price and net asset value, are listed every Monday in *The Wall Street Journal* and every week in *Barron's*. Examples of popular bond funds include: First Boston Strategic Income Fund (NYSE: symbol FBI), High Income Trust (NYSE: YLD), High Yield Income Fund (NYSE: HYI managed by Prudential Insurance), CIM High Yield Fund (AMEX: CIM), Van Kampen Merritt Intermediate Income Fund (NYSE: VIT), and Putnam Master Income Fund (NYSE: PMT).

The minimums on these closed-end bond funds are low. Most sell for under $10 a share, which means that a round lot (100 shares) can be obtained for less than $1,000. You can buy them through any broker.

Of course, as with any bond fund, the price of these closed-end bond funds can vary with interest rates and the economy. Many funds plummeted in the late 1980s but recovered substantially in the early 1990s.

## MUNICIPAL BOND FUNDS

*Muni bond funds* were extremely popular in the 1980s because they held their value as interest rates declined. However, their return fell substantially in the early 1990s, to under 4 percent. The minimum investment for individual munis is $5,000, but the minimum is lower for muni bond funds. We recommend:

Vanguard Municipal Bond Funds
P.O. Box 2600
Valley Forge, PA 19482
800-662-7447

Vanguard offers five different tax-free funds of varying maturities. The high-yield and long-term bond funds pay the highest monthly income. All the funds offer monthly income programs and check-writing privileges.

Investors often overlook the advantages of tax-free closed-end mutual funds. Consider, for example, Summit Tax Exempt Bond Fund (AMEX: SUA), which recently yielded around 7 percent tax free. That's substantially more than most tax-free income funds. The Summit portfolio consists of 11 first-mortgage municipal housing bonds, with an estimated net asset value (NAV) of $16. The price of Summit is substantially below its NAV because the fund holds illiquid real estate units. Nevertheless, the real estate units are almost fully rented and make regular payments.

## CONVERTIBLE BOND FUNDS

There are several convertible bond funds. You can spread your ownership among many different bonds by using such a vehicle. For convenience and diversification, you might want to consider a closed-end convertible bond fund that trades on the Big Board. Putnam High Income Convertible Fund (NYSE: PCF) has had a double-digit yield in the past couple of years and pays monthly income. It also has the potential to increase with the stock market. A round lot of 100 shares costs less than $1,000.

## UTILITY INCOME FUNDS

Utility stocks, poor performers during the inflationary 1970s, rebounded during the past decade. Many utilities, in addition to paying outstanding yields, have doubled in value. No one knows when the trend will end, but, in the meantime, many utilities are still paying dividends of 5 percent or more.

It is extremely important that you buy a diversified group of utilities. It's unlikely that any public utility is going to file for bankruptcy, but the price of a stock could drop sharply or the company could omit its dividend if it has financial trouble or if (as in the case of nuclear utilities) one of its power plants has to be shut down. Don't be fooled by the high yields that some utilities are paying—it may be a premium for a troubled company.

For the small investor, the best alternative is a utility fund. Fidelity offers a no-load utility fund:

> Fidelity Utilities Income Fund
> Devonshire St.
> Boston, MA 02109
> 800-544-8888

This fund is currently yielding 5% and pays monthly dividends.

## ADJUSTABLE-RATE FUNDS AND PRIME-RATE FUNDS

In Chapter 7, we discussed adjustable-rate and prime-rate funds as alternative income sources. Since these funds have become available, they have yielded an average two percentage points more than money funds and T-bills, while maintaining a fairly stable net asset value.

## SHORT-TERM GLOBAL INCOME FUNDS

Another alternative growing in popularity is *short-term global income funds.* These funds invest in foreign money market instruments, including Euro certificates of deposits and short-term bonds. They take advantage of higher interest rates in Europe and the Far East.

The major risk of these funds is the fluctuation in currency exchange. If the dollar falls against major currencies, the fund's value rises. But if the dollar rallies, the fund will decline in value. The principal is not guaranteed to remain stable as it is for money funds.

One fund that has attempted to hedge the currency risk is the Blanchard Short-Term Global Income Fund (see Chapter 7).

## INCOME FROM REAL ESTATE

There are a variety of ways to earn high income from real estate without actually purchasing property, including: Ginnie Mae funds, second mortgages and real estate investment trusts (REITs). Let's take a closer look at each one.

### Ginnie Maes

In 1970, interest rates started rising. Money for home mortgages was difficult to obtain, and the credit crunch threatened the housing and building industry. To encourage investors to lend money to potential homeowners, Congress established the Government National Mortgage Association (GNMA, or Ginnie Mae). Investors could pool their money by buying GNMA certificates, and the money would then be loaned to individual home buyers. The investors didn't have to worry about default on the loans because the principal and interest were guaranteed by the Government National Mortgage Association, the Federal Housing Administration (FHA) or the Department of Veterans Affairs (VA).

Ginnie Mae certificates, now as then, can be a good conservative investment. They are safe and offer a higher rate of return than CDs or money market funds, but the minimum investment is $25,000.

Another drawback to Ginnie Maes is the length of time to maturity. The term on a $25,000 certificate is about 30 years. While it is possible to resell your certificate through your broker before it matures, you can lose money if interest rates have risen because you will have to sell at a discount in order to find a buyer.

These funds can be very volatile. A 1 percent change in interest rate can change the price of a typical Ginnie Mae by about 6 percent. Ginnie Maes are an attractive investment if you can afford the initial investment, if their times to maturity pose no problem to you and if you believe interest rates are likely to fall or remain relatively stable. If interest rates rise, however, the value of your investment will drop.

There is a way to avoid these barriers, though. Ginnie Mae mutual funds exist, which invest primarily in Ginnie Mae certificates, U.S. Treasury obligations and other mortgage-backed securities to diversify. As interest rates on CDs and money market funds have fallen, the popularity of these funds has risen.

There are at least a dozen investment firms offering Ginnie Mae funds. Minimum investment is typically between $1,000 and $3,000, and all earnings can be automatically reinvested.

The following are two no-load Ginnie Mae funds:

Vanguard GNMA Portfolio
P.O. Box 2600
Valley Forge, PA 19482
800-662-7447, 215-648-6000 (in PA)

Benham GNMA Income Fund
1665 Charleston Rd.
Mountain View, CA 94043
800-472-3389

## Second Mortgages

Banks and other lending institutions offer second mortgages to new buyers who need to bridge the gap between their down payment and an assumable loan or to current homeowners who want to borrow against the equity in their homes. Some homeowners unable to qualify for a loan or who prefer not to deal with the bank will often turn to their real estate broker to help them find a private lender. And that's where you can come in. You can let several brokers know that you have money available for second mortgages, and they will call you when a client needs money.

How is a typical second mortgage structured? You can set

up any terms that are agreeable to both lender and borrower. Typically, the second mortgage will be amortized as though it were a 30-year loan, to keep payments lower, with a balloon payment for the balance after five years.

You can charge any interest rate that both you and the borrower agree to, as long as it does not exceed any usury laws your state may impose. ("Usury" is the practice of lending money at an excessively high interest rate.) Generally, the greater the risk and the stronger the client's need, the higher the interest rate will be on second mortgages. You can also buy a discounted existing second mortgage from a current lender. When you buy a discounted mortgage, you can expect to pay about 5 percent less than the face value, or remaining balance, on the loan for each year remaining on the note. For example, you could buy a $10,000 note for $9,500 if it has one year remaining, or for $8,000 if there are four years to go. The borrower continues to pay you the full amount, so you will earn capital gains as well as interest.

One risk you face, and your biggest concern, is that the borrower may default on the loan. If the homeowner has a $100,000 house (conservatively appraised for current market value) and owes $60,000 on the first mortgage, you could safely lend up to $20,000 on a second mortgage. This gives you a $20,000 cushion to protect yourself against a quick sale at a below-market price or against a federal tax lien. (Uncle Sam's claims come first, followed by the first mortgage, then the second. Repair liens, utilities and other clients come next.)

On the other hand, if the homeowner already owes $90,000 on the first mortgage and wants to borrow $20,000, half of your investment will be totally unprotected. Since the homeowner will have no equity in the house (in fact, he will owe more than the house is worth), he could easily be tempted to walk away from his obligations and let it go into foreclosure. Because your risk in this situation is so much greater, you can charge a much higher interest rate—if you decide to grant the loan.

Another risk in granting second mortgages is that you might need to regain your capital before the loan expires. In that case, you will have to find another lender willing to "buy your paper," and you will have to sell at a discount, meaning that you will receive less than the amount you originally lent.

What if the borrower defaults—have you lost it all? There is still a way to save your investment, and perhaps profit even more: You can assume the first mortgage, often with no assumption fees and no down payment, and become full owner of the house.

A subscriber used this technique to turn a bad loan into a valuable asset. It cost her $1,100 to gain title to the house. She assumed the first mortgage and eliminated the second, since she was now both lender and borrower. Three months later, she sold the house for a $15,000 profit.

How can you earn high interest and still limit your risks?

Know your borrower. Insist that the real estate broker or other middle person provide you with a complete financial disclosure statement.

Make sure the loan is secured by more than promises. You can earn a higher return on a no-equity loan, but you risk losing your entire investment.

Select a borrower who has enough cash value in the house to give him an incentive to keep up the payments, and whose house is located in a good neighborhood. Check local records for any liens from taxes, unpaid utility bills or construction loans. Be prepared to take over the mortgage payment if foreclosure seems imminent and either rent the house or try to resell it.

For more information about second mortgages, contact the Mortgage Bankers Association, 1125 15th St., N.W., Washington, D.C. 20005, 202-861-6500.

## Real Estate Investment Trusts

Real estate investment trusts (REITs) are mutual funds that invest in real estate. They allow small investors to participate in the profits of owning shopping centers, office buildings, apartment complexes, hotels, warehouses and even race tracks, for example. REITs are an easy, convenient and profitable way to invest in real estate without having to buy property. Over a hundred REITs are traded publicly on the stock exchange, offering you liquidity not available with direct property ownership.

There are basically two kinds of REITs: equity and mortgage. *Equity REITs* own property outright. Dividends are paid from rental income, and capital gains are passed on to the shareholder in the form of special dividends or increased earnings when properties are sold. Investors can also get tax benefits from depreciation of the properties. *Mortgage REITs* do not own property outright but make mortgage loans for property owners. They are riskier because assets are intangible—if the property owner defaults, the REIT may lose, like any other mortgage lender. But while mortgage REITs are riskier, they also pay more.

Your principal is not guaranteed when you invest in a real estate trust. If a property turns out to be in a poor location and suffers from chronic vacancies, for example, dividends will be reduced and the value of shares will drop. If interest rates rise while a REIT is locked into lower-paying mortgages, this could also reduce share values.

Clearly, you must be careful in choosing a REIT that will maintain its value. Read the prospectus carefully, paying special attention to the sections detailing the properties that are owned or will be owned. If a property is still being built, study the location, market demand and developer's track record before investing.

What kind of REIT is best for you? If you need current income, a mortgage REIT generally pays the highest yield. If you want to buy your shares through your retirement fund, choose a high-yielding mortgage REIT, since interest income is tax deferred inside your pension fund. (If you put an equity REIT into your tax-deferred fund, you will lose the tax advantages of the REIT.)

A mutual fund that specializes in REITs is the United Services Real Estate Fund (800-873-8637 or 512-696-1234). A closed-end REIT that invests in discounted RTC loans is Allied Capital Commercial Corp. (NASDAQ: ALCC).

For more information on REITs, contact a broker, or contact the National Association of Real Estate Investment Trusts, 1129 20th St., N.W., Suite 705, Washington, DC 20036, 202-785-8717.

## WRITING CALL OPTIONS ON BLUE-CHIP STOCKS

Blue-chip stocks, such as the 30 Dow Jones industrials, pay healthy dividends several times a year, although their yields are not normally as high as that paid on bonds. Investors don't invest in blue-chip stocks solely for income, however; they are usually more interested in seeing the price of the stock grow.

Many stockbrokers have recommended writing "call options" on the blue-chip stocks that customers own as a way to increase the return on their stocks. The term may seem complicated to the novice investor, but options are really quite simple.

In the stock-option market, investors can buy or sell the right to purchase a stock at a future date at a specified price. Suppose the current price of a certain stock is $30, and an investor thinks the price will rise within the next six months. He would buy a call option, which would allow him to buy 100 shares of that stock at any time in the next six months at the "strike price" he chooses (let's say the current $30). If the price goes up, he will exercise the option, but if it remains the same or drops, the option will expire worthless. Thus, the buyer of a call option is speculating on the short-term price of the stock.

So how does this increase your yield? Suppose you own 100 shares of a stock selling at $30 a share and paying a 5 percent dividend. You think the price will remain stable, so you sell a call option through your broker to a speculator who thinks it will rise. Let's say you received $360 for the sale of the option. On $3,000 worth of stock, that's an additional 12 percent return, making your total return, with your continued 5 percent dividend, 17 percent.

If the price of the stock rises to, say, $50 during the next six months, the speculator who bought the option exercises the option and buys $5,000 worth of the stock (100 shares × $50) for $3,000 because he locked in a price of $30 when he purchased your option—not bad for his $360 investment. On the other hand, if the price drops to $10, he will let the option expire, and his $360 purchase will have saved him the loss of $2,000.

While writing the call option may have cost you the opportunity to earn big profits if the price rose, it also protected part of your capital if the price fell. No matter what, your principal investment remains the same, and you have greatly increased your yield while letting someone else gamble on the short-term price movement of the stock.

An excellent no-load fund that writes options on the largest 100 U.S. stocks is Gateway Index Plus Fund, 400 Technecenter Dr., Suite 220, Milford, OH 45150, 800-354-6339. Minimum investment is $1,000.

## NATURAL RESOURCE STOCKS, GOLD SHARES AND LIMITED PARTNERSHIPS

Investments in mining, oil and gas, and natural resources have often paid handsome dividends.

In the 1970s, South African gold stocks paid dividends exceeding 15 percent. Since 1980, however, South African dividends have gradually eroded and are now paying less than 10 percent.

An exception has been the South African utility bonds, known as ESKOM bonds, which have yielded 18 to 20 percent recently. If you want more information, contact Barry Downs, Noyes Securities in New Jersey, 800-835-5647, 201-402-8022. These bonds are volatile, due to the political situation in South Africa. Minimum investment is $10,000.

North American mining stocks have traditionally paid little in dividends, with the exception of Freeport McMoRan Copper and Gold (NYSE: FCX). The dividend yield on that stock has been between 4 to 5 percent. Otherwise, North American gold stocks typically pay 1 to 2 percent in dividends, hardly a decent income source.

Limited partnerships in oil and gas, fertilizer, real estate and other natural resources have had a checkered history. Some have doubled and tripled in value; others have fallen on hard times. High returns and high risk seem to go hand in hand.

Freeport McMoRan of New Orleans is one of the largest natural resource companies in the world. In addition to the copper-gold mining operation, they also have worldwide investments in oil and gas, fertilizer, and mining. Freeport McMoRan Resources Master Partnership (NYSE: FRP) has been a decent performer so far, with a double-digit yield, which is partly tax deferred. The partnership is a major fertilizer producer and has an interest in a sizable oil and gas field as well. You can also sell options on the stock for additional income.

One broker familiar with natural resource stocks and partnerships is Rick Rule, Torrey Pines Securities, 140 Marine View Dr., Suite 110, Solana Beach, CA 92075, 800-688-8679. Small accounts are welcome.

## ANNUITIES AND OTHER INSURANCE PRODUCTS

Annuities are a popular source of monthly income. Many retirees, for example, will convert their IRAs or other pension funds into an annuity and receive monthly income for the rest of their lives. Or they can make a lump-sum payment to the insurance company in exchange for a lifetime income. The amount they receive depends on how much they invested, as well as their age and life expectancy. There are a variety of plans available from insurance companies. We would recommend dealing only with top-rated companies (those that are rated highest by reliable rating agencies such as A. M. Best & Co. and Standard & Poor's).

For an annuity specialist, contact one of our recommended independent insurance agents: David T. Phillips & Co., 3200 N. Dobson Rd., Bldg. C, Chandler, AZ 85224, 800-223-9610, 602-897-6088.

### What about Swiss Annuities?

Foreign annuities, denominated in Swiss francs, German marks or other currencies, have also been popular among American retirees seeking protection against inflation and a weak dollar.

U.S. annuities don't normally provide inflationary protection at retirement. If you are paid $1,000 a month, you'll still get $1,000 a month a decade from now, even though consumer prices may have doubled. Therefore, American investors have looked to the annuities sold in stable countries, such as Switzerland, that promise long-term economic security and low inflation.

The Swiss franc was worth 23 cents in 1970. Today, it's worth over 70 cents. How does this affect your retirement income? Suppose in 1970 you bought a Swiss annuity that paid 4,310 Swiss francs each month, then equivalent to $1,000, for the rest of your life. Today you'd still receive 4,310 francs a month, but how much would it be worth in dollars? At today's rate of exchange, about $3,000.

The Swiss franc has done well against the dollar and other currencies in the past (see Figure 10.1). Will it appreciate against the dollar in the future? It all depends on the policies of both the United States and Switzerland. If the Swiss maintain an anti-inflation policy while the United States is highly inflationary, we believe the Swiss franc annuity will provide some protection. But

**Figure 10.1**

Swiss Franc Appreciation, 1970–1990

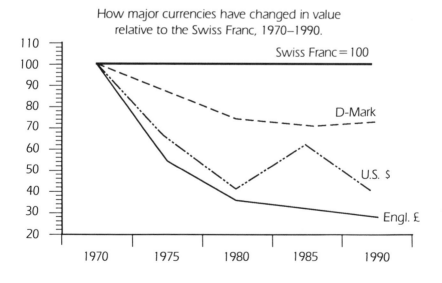

How major currencies have changed in value relative to the Swiss Franc, 1970–1990.

be aware that the Swiss franc lost value against the dollar for nearly seven years (1978–85) because of the strong dollar and because of President Reagan's anti-inflation policies. It's difficult to predict the value of currencies, even over long periods of time. Our conclusion is that you use a Swiss franc annuity as a supplement to U.S. annuities, but don't depend on it for all your retirement needs.

For information on Swiss annuities, write to:

JML Swiss Investment Counsellors
Germaniastrasse 55
8033 Zurich, Switzerland
Telephone (011-411) 363-2510

## Private Annuities

Private annuities are another interesting financial alternative. Suppose you are ready to retire and need additional monthly income. You may decide to sell your home to one of your children, who will then pay you a "private annuity" each month instead of a lump-sum payment. You receive a monthly check for the rest of your life, the amount of which is determined by your age, the market price of the house and the insurance tables. Meanwhile, you may continue to live in the house if you wish. When you die, the house will already belong to your heirs and will not be part of your taxable estate. No further payments will be due to your heirs. For more information on private annuities, contact an attorney.

## THE DILEMMA FACING INCOME-SEEKERS

The income-seeker faces a difficult decision. You can stay with low monthly income from safe bank CDs or money market funds, or you can venture into high-yielding bonds, utilities, natural resource stocks, and foreign annuities but face the possibility that your principal will lose value. Those investors who are on limited budgets and who need monthly income may have to reexamine their financial goals. A steady, high monthly income that keeps up with inflation is elusive. To stay ahead of the game—to find those "high-growth, high-income" alternatives— the income-seeker may have to speculate in some riskier invest- ments.

# CHAPTER 11

# The Beginner's Guide to International Investing

*Great estates may venture more; little boats must keep to shore.*

—Poor Richard's Almanac

$A$ BOOK ON HIGH FINANCE would not be complete without a survey of investment opportunities around the world. For years wealthy investors have taken advantage of booming stock markets in London, Paris, Zurich, Tokyo, Mexico City and Hong Kong. They have bought and sold art and collectibles in major European cities. They have established Swiss bank accounts and taken advantage of the celebrated ability of the "Swiss gnomes" to manage money and minimize taxes.

Such global opportunities are now available to every investor, not just the sophisticated, well-heeled, private investor. In the past decade, the financial revolution has spread around the world, and with free markets developing everywhere, now is the time to get aboard.

It's time for all investors, especially small investors who want to build their wealth quickly, to look north, south, east and west. While the U.S. stock market may rise 30 percent in a year, foreign stock markets may double or triple! The following graph, Figure 11.1, demonstrates the possibilities. During the last half of the 1980s, seven major stock markets outperformed the U.S., even when the U.S. had an outstanding bull market. Japan, Austria, Singapore and Germany outdistanced the U.S. market by three to one or more. And, in the early 1990s, while Wall Street performed admirably, the stock markets in Mexico, Argentina, Chile and other emerging markets were doubling and tripling in value.

Of course, the world's stock markets can be treacherous, too. Wall Street crashed in 1987, and Tokyo crashed in 1990. The long term may be bullish, but the short term may be dubious.

**Figure 11.1**

World Stock Index Outperforms U.S. Market

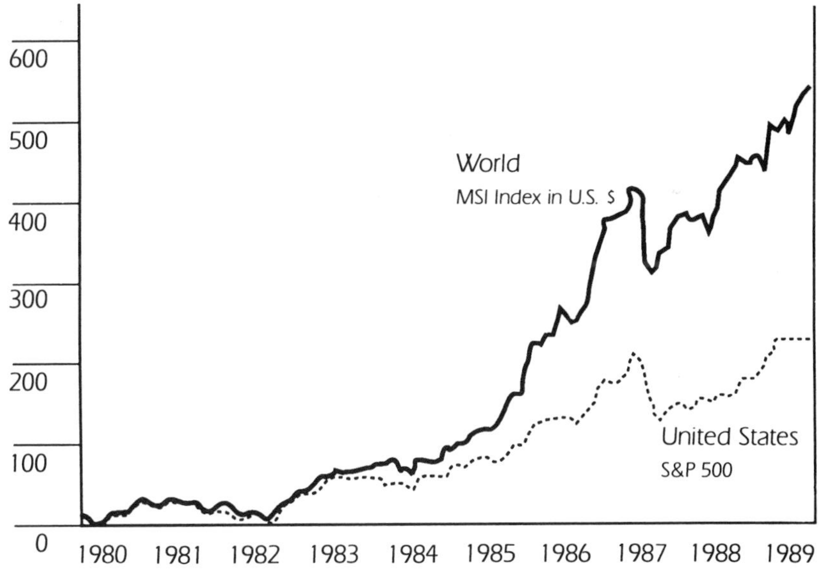

World
MSI Index in U.S. $

United States
S&P 500

0    1980    1981    1982    1983    1984    1985    1986    1987    1988    1989

Source: Union Bank of Switzerland

So how does the small investor get involved in the global investment marketplace? In the past, it was not easy. A few hundred foreign stocks could be purchased directly on the New York Stock

Exchange or over the counter (OTC). These specially registered foreign stocks are known as American Depository Receipts, or ADRs. But it required expert guidance to put together a diversified portfolio, and most brokers were not that familiar with foreign markets. Sophisticated investors had their money managed overseas by a London or Swiss banker, who was not limited to ADRs.

John Templeton made it convenient to invest globally when he began his famous Templeton Growth Fund in 1954, which invested in foreign as well as domestic stocks. Despite its high load fee (8.5 percent), it has performed extremely well.

Now, of course, there are literally dozens of ways for the small investor to profit from spectacular foreign markets. Let's look at some of them.

## INTERNATIONAL MUTUAL FUNDS

Today there are numerous mutual funds that specialize in foreign stocks. Many of these funds are no-load or closed-end funds that trade on major stock exchanges. In today's world, there is little need to send your money abroad to invest in foreign markets. You can do it simply by making a local telephone call to your broker, or by calling a family of funds with an 800 number.

Here are two no-load international funds that *Forbes* has ranked as solid performers:

T. Rowe Price International Stock Fund
100 East Pratt St.
Baltimore, MD 21202
800-638-5660

Scudder International Fund
160 Federal St.
Boston, MA 02110
800-225-2470

You can buy either fund directly from the addresses above, or through a discount broker, such as Charles Schwab & Co. or Jack White & Co.

Load funds that have performed well over the years include the Templeton Foreign Fund (8.5 percent load) and the GT International Growth Fund (4.75 percent load). It is best to buy these load funds through a broker. Sometimes you can negotiate a reduction in the load, depending on the size of your investment and your relationship with the broker.

## COUNTRY FUNDS

One of the most popular ways to invest abroad is to select a mutual fund that specializes in one country. This way you can invest in a "hot" country, then switch to another when the international climate changes. There always seems to be a hot stock market somewhere around the world and, with dozens of country funds, you are able to invest in them when they are moving up.

Most country funds are closed-end and trade on a stock exchange. The big exception is the Japan Fund, which is now an open-ended fund managed by Scudder.

Here is a list of well-known country and regional funds that you may want to discuss with your broker:

*Latin America.* Mexico Fund (NYSE: MXF), Chile Fund (NYSE: CH), Brazil Fund (NYSE: BZF), Argentina Fund (NYSE: AF) and the Latin American Fund (NYSE: LAF).

*Europe.* Germany Fund (NYSE: GER), Italy Fund (NYSE: ITA), Austria Fund (NYSE: ST), Spain Fund (NYSE: SNF) and the GT Greater Europe Fund (NYSE: GTF).

*Far East.* Japan OTC Equity Fund (NYSE: JOF), Taiwan Fund (NYSE: TWN), Korea Fund (NYSE: KF), Singapore Fund (NYSE: SGF) and the Scudder New Asia Fund (NYSE: SAF).

There are, of course, many other country and region funds.

Check *Barron's* for a complete listing or *Morningstar Closed-End Fund Survey*.

You can buy any of these country funds through a broker. Imagine buying a diversified investment in a faraway country for around $1,000!

## EMERGING MARKETS

The collapse of socialist central planning in Eastern Europe and the Soviet Union in the late 1980s has created a new impetus for the development of free-enterprise capitalism in many parts of the world. Former socialist regimes are now experimenting with privatization and other free-market reforms. New stock markets are being established, offering opportunities to make money in emerging Third World countries for the first time.

Top money managers are well aware of this new trend toward a global free market and have established mutual funds specializing in emerging markets. The two best-known funds are the Templeton Emerging Markets Fund (NYSE: EMF) and the Morgan Stanley Emerging Markets Fund (NYSE: MSF). Here is your opportunity to get in on the ground floor in Africa, Asia, Europe and Latin America as they adopt free-enterprise capitalism.

## HIGH-INTEREST FOREIGN BONDS

In the early 1980s, U.S. interest rates skyrocketed while European and other foreign interest rates stayed relatively low. By the early 1990s, the trend reversed itself. Interest rates fell to low levels in the United States, while they skyrocketed in Europe and Japan. U.S. investors can take advantage of high interest rates abroad by investing in foreign bonds and international certificates of deposit. Several mutual funds specialize in these markets. No-load funds include T. Rowe Price International Bond Fund (800-638-5660) and Scudder International Bond Fund (800-225-2470).

A good performing load fund is PaineWebber Global Income Fund (800-225-2385). The Blanchard Short-Term Global Income Fund (800-688-7904) seeks to minimize currency risks by hedging its account.

Also, if you are seeking income from foreign sources, don't forget the advantages of Swiss annuities, discussed in Chapter 10.

## INVESTING THROUGH A FOREIGN BANK

So far we've discussed ways in which the small investor can begin investing internationally through a U.S. broker or mutual fund. Some investors may wish to venture further by opening a foreign bank account and investing abroad directly. There are several advantages to this approach: First, you can invest in a wider variety of individual foreign stocks and foreign mutual funds (known as *unit investment trusts*). Second, you can place some assets and investment funds outside the direct control of the U.S. government.

Most foreign banks impose rather high minimums on U.S. customers. Typically you need $25,000 or more to open an account with a major Swiss or European bank. However, there are some exceptions. Consider these banks:

• *Lloyds Bank's "High Interest Cheque Account."* Lloyds Bank is one of the largest banks in the world. It offers a unique checking account that pays interest ranging from 1.5 to 7.5 percent. You receive a Lloyds checkbook, a special Visa card that allows you to make purchases anywhere in the world and a cash-withdrawal card. The account is denominated in British pounds. Minimum investment is $2,500. Larger amounts are required if you wish to buy and sell securities. For information, write Lloyds Banks, 39 Threadneedle St., London EC2R 8AU, England.

• *Ueberseebank* is a medium-sized Swiss bank geared for the small investor. Minimum investment to open a Swiss franc savings account is $3,000. Ueberseebank also offers accounts in stocks and bonds, mutual funds, precious metals, and managed accounts. For information, contact Ueberseebank, Limmatquai 2, CH-8024 Zurich, Switzerland.

• *Royal Trust Bank (Austria)*, located in Vienna, Austria, is a favorite of small investors. Royal Trust Bank is owned by Royal Trust of Canada, one of the largest financial institutions in the world. Minimum investment to open an account is $3,000. Royal Trust Austria specializes in buying and selling mutual funds, charging only 1 percent commission. It also offers accounts in stocks, bonds, certificates of deposit, precious metals, and bearer passbook savings accounts. For information, write the Royal Trust Bank (Austria), P.O. Box A-1011, Vienna, Austria.

• *Hong Kong & Shanghai Bank* offers the most flexible and high-yielding multicurrency accounts in the world. Its CombiNations Savings Accounts are offered in ten different currencies, including the Swiss franc, German mark, U.S. dollar and Japanese yen. Minimum investment is $1,000. For more information, write CombiNations Savings Accounts, Hong Kong & Shanghai Bank, 1 Queen's Road Central, Hong Kong.

## OFFSHORE UNIT INVESTMENT TRUSTS

There are thousands of foreign mutual funds that are not registered in the U.S. and do not trade on American exchanges. Yet many of them have track records far superior to those of U. S. funds. A full listing of these mutual funds, or *unit investment trusts,* as they are called, is published daily in the *Financial Times.* The *Financial Times* is published in London but is available in major cities in the United States (800-628-8088).

You can buy these mutual funds through the foreign banks listed above.

## INVESTING OVERSEAS IS THE WAVE OF THE FUTURE

In sum, you can profit handsomely from global investing, whether you have $1,000 or $100,000. You can open a small savings account in any major currency. You can invest in "hot" country funds or purchase individual foreign stocks. You can store gold and silver outside the country in a Swiss bank account. You can earn high income abroad.

Diversification is the watchword in these uncertain times. It pays to have a portion of your nest egg in foreign investments, to protect your assets and to profit from new global opportunities.

# CHAPTER 12

# The Small Investor's Gold Mine

*Genius without education is like silver in the mine.*

—Poor Richard's Almanac

Throughout history, gold has been universally recognized as a measure of money. Battles have been fought over it, the Americas were settled in search of it, and as long as the dollar was tied to it, we had a fairly stable economy. The value of gold will endure long after the last note of paper money has been used for fireplace kindling.

During times of raging inflation, gold and silver can make a handsome profit for the investor with foresight. During social upheaval, such as that experienced in Nazi Germany or communist Vietnam, it can mean life or death, as many people have traded metals for escape. During natural disaster or wartime strife, it can provide food for your table. And during those occasional lulls when the economy looks good and life seems fair, it can give a continued sense of security, providing a backup for bad times.

But precious metals cannot be considered a consistent profitmaker. In many ways, gold and silver should be treated like an

insurance policy—a necessary expense in case disaster (or inflation) strikes, but not a primary investment for all economic cli-
mates.

During the 1970s, when inflation was high and real interest
rates (relative to the inflation rate) were low, gold investments did
well while conservative stocks and bonds did poorly. In the past
decade, however, inflation dropped and precious metals were
poor investments.

Figure 12.1 illustrates how the price of gold has fluctuated
during the past decade. Note that the price didn't increase steadily, in a straight line, but moved up in cyclical fashion. It tended to
move up sharply when inflation accelerated (as in the 1970s) but
dropped off when inflation subsided (as in the 1980s).

**Figure 12.1**

Gold Prices, 1982–1992

## GOLD BULLION COINS

No investment portfolio can be considered complete without the
inclusion of a few gold and silver coins. Coins are the easiest
and most popular way to invest in gold and silver. Coins are

immediately identifiable, they are generally accepted without being assayed, they are small enough to be carried in your pocket and you can legally move them in and out of the country without having to report them.

Gold coins come in various sizes, from over one ounce to as small as one-tenth of an ounce. However, the best buy is the one-ounce coin because you will pay a smaller premium for it than for the smaller coins. In the United States, the American Eagles are a popular way to buy gold in one-ounce sizes. Other popular gold coins are the Canadian Maple Leaf (one troy ounce), the Austrian 100 Corona (0.9802 ounce) and the Mexican 50 peso (1.2056 ounce). The South African Krugerrand (one troy ounce) used to be the most popular gold coin, but it fell out of favor in the 1980s. These are bullion coins, meaning that their price is determined by the daily spot price of gold quoted on the major exchanges. They are minted in huge quantities and do not have any numismatic, or rarity, value. Typically you will pay a premium over the gold content of the coin of 3 to 4 percent.

## COMMON-DATED GOLD COINS AND MEDALLIONS

The U.S. Treasury discontinued minting U.S. gold coins in 1933. It was also in 1933 that it became illegal for Americans to own gold. Collectible coins and medallions were an exception, however, and hobbyists continued to trade the $20 Double Eagle, $10 Eagle and $5 Half-Eagle. Even after the gold ban was lifted in 1975, these U.S. coins continued to be a popular investment, although prices have fluctuated. The market is very liquid in common-dated Eagles, and they are a good way to profit from both gold prices and collector demand. They should definitely be included in your coin portfolio.

The U.S. government did not mint any gold coins again until 1980, when they began minting commemorative medallions and legal-tender coins, and the new American Eagles in 1986. These have met with varying degrees of success. Hundreds of thousands of the medallions were eventually melted down because no one wanted to buy them, although a few have more than doubled in price. We will cover the rare-coin market more fully in Chapter 13, when we discuss collectibles.

## BUYING GOLD BULLION

There are several ways to invest in precious metals, including bullion bars, bullion coins, rare coins and futures contracts.

Gold bullion bars are available in several sizes, including the standard 400-ounce bar, 100 ounces, 10 ounces, 5 ounces and even 1 ounce. Bars are sold by major refiners and banks, such as Swiss Credit Bank and the Bank of Nova Scotia.

A small investor can purchase a one-ounce gold bullion bar for about 10 percent premium over the actual gold price, but we don't recommend that you do this because bullion bars are often hard to sell and an assaying fee is often required to determine the genuine content of the bar.

Gold bullion may be worth purchasing, however. If you view it purely as an investment and allow a reputable bank or gold dealer to hold it for you, it is an excellent, convenient way to invest in gold. Transactions can be negotiated instantly, often by phone, and sometimes even faster than buying or selling coins.

During the frenzied bull market of gold during 1979–80, many coin dealers and banks refused to give quotes over the phone or over the counter. You couldn't buy and you couldn't sell your gold or silver coins for a period of time because of the volatility of prices. But if you had bought gold bullion and had it held for you by Citibank, Merrill Lynch or Swiss Credit Bank, you could still have sold that gold instantly, based on the London price fix for gold on that particular day. This is an instance in which gold bullion was more liquid than gold coins!

## SILVER COINS: POOR MAN'S GOLD

Silver has traditionally sold for considerably less than the yellow metal, and it is often called the poor man's gold. However, silver has been much more volatile than gold because it's more an industrial metal. In 1970, silver bullion sold for around $1.65 an ounce. By 1980, it had reached a new high of nearly $50.00 an ounce, and it has since dropped to under $5.00. Figure 12.2 shows the change in the price of silver from 1982 to 1992.

**Figure 12.2**

Silver Prices, 1982–1992

Silver coins are the best medium for small investors who want to get into precious metals. U.S. silver dimes, quarters, half-dollars and dollars that were minted prior to 1965 are often referred to as "junk" silver—but this junk may be a real treasure. By 1965, the value of silver used in minting coins exceeded the face value of the coins, and consequently, they became collector's items.

The small investor's best bet is to buy "junk" silver dimes, quarters, half-dollars or dollars. We would avoid the Kennedy and Eisenhower 40 percent coins, which were minted from 1965–70, except as a novelty. If you're buying for silver content only, not for the beauty or rarity of the coin, "junk" silver offers you the best value because it's available at the lowest premium.

Silver coins can be bought in any quantity. The most expensive, but the best value, is a bag of coins whose face value totals

$1,000. You can also purchase half-bags ($500 face value), quarter-bags ($250 face value) and tenth-bags ($100 face value).

Table 12.1 shows the pure silver content of silver coins. All U.S. pre-1964 coins were 90 percent silver.

**Table 12.1**

U.S. Silver Coins

| | Pure Silver Content (Troy ounces) |
|---|---|
| Dimes, 1916–64 | .07234 oz. |
| Quarters, 1916–64 | .18084 oz. |
| Half-Dollars, 1916–64 | .36169 oz. |
| Kennedy 40% Silver Half-Dollars, 1965–70 | .14792 oz. |
| Peace & Morgan Dollars 1878–1935 | .77344 oz. |
| Eisenhower 40% Silver Dollars, 1971–76 (Proof only) | .31625 oz. |

Rolls of coins can fit easily into the small investor's portfolio. Dimes come in rolls of 50 with a face value of $5, while quarters are packed 40 to a roll and have a $10 face value.

## WHERE TO BUY AT THE LOWEST PRICE

The markets for gold and silver coins fluctuate, and prices may vary considerably among coin dealers. It pays to shop around, especially when the markets become volatile.

*Silver & Gold Report,* a monthly precious metals newsletter, surveys major coin dealers every six months and ranks them according to their prices for various gold and silver coins. For the latest survey, send $10 to *Silver & Gold Report,* P.O. Box 2923, West Palm Beach, FL 33402.

Below are the addresses and toll-free numbers of coin dealers that usually rank highly in the *Silver & Gold Report* survey. Get a quote for the coins you wish to buy from each of them. Be sure to call all of them at about the same time since prices vary during the day. And be sure to ask for the full delivered price.

- Benham Certified Metals, 1665 Charleston Rd., Mountain View, CA 94043, 800-447-4653 or 415/965-4275.

- Camino Coin, 875 Mahler Rd., Suite 150, Burlingame, CA 94010, 800-348-8001 or 415-348-3000.

- Dillon Gage, Inc., 15301 Dallas Pkwy., Suite 200, Dallas, TX 75248, 800-537-2583 or 214-788-4765.

- Rhyne Precious Metals, 425 Pike St., Suite 403, Seattle, WA 98101, 800-426-7835 or 206-623-6900.

- Sam Sloat, Inc., P.O. Box 192, 606 Post Rd. E., Westport, CT 06881, 800-243-5670 or 203-226-4279.

- SilverTowne, P.O. Box 424, Route 4, Old Union City Pike, Winchester, IN 47394, 800-788-7481 or 317-584-7481.

## GOLD MINING STOCKS

Gold shares offer the chance to make highly leveraged gains while earning some dividends. If the price of gold rises 10 percent, some gold stocks may rise 50 percent. Gold shares have always been regarded as speculative, providing the chance to make lucrative gains—or suffer big losses. Gold stocks do not always move with the price of gold, although over the long run they are tied together. Some gold stocks may rise sharply even though the price of gold is stable. A mining company may discover a new property, or new management may take over and improve the mining operation.

The gold mining industry has experienced a major revolution over the past twenty years. In fact, there is only one gold mining company in North America today that existed under the same name 20 years ago—Homestake Mining Company. Today the big mining companies include American Barrick (NYSE: ABX), Newmont Mining (NYSE: NEM), Pegasus Gold (ASE: PGU) and Placer Dome (NYSE: PDG). Benham offers an index fund representing the top 30 gold mining companies in North America: Benham Gold Equities Index Fund (800-472-3389).

South African gold stocks include Kloof, Western Deep, and Driefontein. ASA is a closed-end fund that specializes in South African mining stocks and trades on the New York Stock Exchange. A no-load fund in South African golds is United Services Gold Shares Fund (800-873-8637). Because of political instability, South African gold stocks are considered more speculative than the North Americans, even though they pay higher dividends.

## SPECULATING IN PENNY MINING SHARES

Penny mining shares are an exciting way to make big profits in a bull market in gold and silver. These low-cost stocks, which sell for between 5 cents and $5 per share, can give you dramatic price appreciation—perhaps increasing tenfold in a bull market. They are very risky, however, as prices can drop as fast as they rise. Commissions and the bid/ask spread can be substantial, and they are not as liquid as the blue-chip stocks trading on the New York Stock Exchange. Penny shares trade on exchanges in Vancouver and Toronto, and over the counter in the United States. They are a risky, long-term investment, and you should only use money you can afford to lose.

There doesn't have to be a major bull market in gold and silver to profit from penny mining stocks. New mines are being discovered all the time, primarily in Nevada, Canada, South America and Asia. Even while the gold market in general is floundering, a new company can skyrocket if a discovery is made.

One of the best newsletters on junior gold shares is *Gold Mining Stock Report*, published by Bob Bishop, P.O. Box 1217, Lafayette, CA 94549, $159 a year.

And for a brokerage firm that specializes in penny shares, contact:

Torrey Pines Securities
140 Marine View Dr., Suite 110
Solana Beach, CA 92075
800-688-8679

## SUMMARY OF GOLD AND SILVER

We have found that small investors can profit from a portfolio in gold and silver bullion, coins and stocks. They can do it conveniently, safely and at low cost. They can buy single gold coins, rolls of silver dimes or higher-priced coins from reputable dealers at a low premium and without paying a sales tax. They can even speculate in exotic gold mining shares with only $500 and without paying sales commissions. In conclusion, the rich aren't so different, after all!

# CHAPTER 13

# $100 Gets You Started in Art and Collectibles

*Wealth is not his that has it, but his that enjoys it.*

—Poor Richard's Almanac

THE HOMES OF THE wealthy are often filled with lovely furnishings and their lives with exotic hobbies that not only bring them pleasure but prove to be profitable investments as well. The person on a low budget, however, has generally settled for cheap copies of period pieces, and such less expensive hobbies as collecting matchbooks or baseball cards, because the prices of antiques, stamps, art and other collectibles were simply too high.

In the inflationary 1970s, collectibles were in a feverish bull market. Salomon Brothers' survey of inflation hedges listed stamps, Chineses ceramics, rare books, diamonds and old masters as just a few of the collectible fields that exploded during that decade of inflation. But during the 1980s, prices of collectibles slowed and even fell, as inflation slowed around the world.

Still, many success stories about collectibles go unreported in the newspapers, stories of lower-priced items that quietly continue to increase in value without any fanfare. By gaining a working knowledge of the subject, even those on the tightest budgets can enter the collectibles market, purchasing items for as little as $100 that may eventually be worth thousands.

Can the small investor really afford to buy genuine antiques and collectibles? Yes! John L. Marion, chairman of Sotheby's, the world's most prestigious auction house, emphatically declares that collecting is for every taste and every budget. In his fascinating book, *The Best of Everything* (Simon & Schuster, 1989), he states, "Certainly, rare and exceptionally fine works are expensive, but it is precisely because they are so rare that this is so. The majority—and this invariably comes as a surprise to the average person—*are quite affordable.*" Marion gives an example: "With the proper guidance, you can have the real thing—like the exquisite eight-foot by four-foot 1920s Persian rug we sold for $1,980, or about half what you might pay at Bloomingdale's or Macy's for a new rug of comparable quality."

Shopping for collectibles can be great fun because it combines consumption with investing. While most investments are stored in vaults or registered on pieces of paper, collectibles can be enjoyed in your home even as they appreciate in value. For example, our son began collecting comic books when he was very young. He selected them wisely, stored them carefully and enjoyed them through his teen years. When it was time for college, his education fund was in his closet rather than the bank.

A friend of his made a similar "investment" in an old car. He restored it, enjoyed it during high school and then sold it at a profit to pay for his first two years of college. He also learned a valuable skill as a mechanic in the process.

You might decide to purchase one good antique, artwork, rare coin or firearm each year. Enjoy them for 20 years or more, and then sell them to pay for your children's tuition or your own retirement. Choosing wisely and avoiding retail prices are the key to this enjoy-as-you-save plan. Still, your primary question should be "Do I like it?" rather than "How much can I sell it for?" This is an investment you will live with and enjoy.

## GETTING STARTED

Knowledge is your most important asset when investing in art and other collectibles. The more you know about what makes an item valuable, the better your chance of finding top quality at a rock-bottom price. You won't find Aladdin's lamp in a junk store unless you know a great deal about Arabian brassworks—and perhaps a little bit about genies as well.

Of course, you can't expect to become an expert on all the art forms and collector's items available—even the professionals rely on one another to specialize. This is the one investment area where diversification is not the key to risk-free speculation. You need to select one specific area that is appealing to you and then learn everything there is to know about it. If you like Oriental rugs, for example, you should eventually be able to determine where one was made just by looking at the design; how it was made by examining the type of knot; when it was made by determining the source of the dyes; and how well it was made by counting the knots per square inch. Additionally, you should keep up to date on current auction prices. All of this information is available at the public library.

## WHERE TO BUY: AUCTIONS VERSUS DEALERS

As you become an expert in your field, you may find someone to deal with locally who is both reasonable and reliable, but at first, our recommendation is to avoid local retail dealers and deal through the large, well-known auction houses. Numismatic coins, old jewelry, antique firearms, rare books and old paintings can easily be overvalued, or even counterfeited, by unscrupulous dealers. This is a field replete with con artists, so you must be constantly on guard. If it sounds too good to be true, it probably is!

These are the names and addresses of two reputable auction houses:

Sotheby's, Inc.
1334 York Ave.
New York, NY 10021
800-444-3709
212-606-7000

Christie's
502 Park Ave.
New York, NY 10022
718-784-1480

Sotheby's and Christie's both publish catalogs throughout the year giving detailed descriptions of what will be available at upcoming auctions. A different catalog is published for each collectible category, such as books, paintings, wines, rugs, autographs, coins, ceramics, etc. You can send for a free list of these catalogs, which will include a detailed breakdown of the categories and the prices charged for each catalog. Sotheby's also publishes a newsletter that announces upcoming auctions and mentions special items that will be featured. The newsletter costs $10 a year.

In addition to describing the items for sale, the catalog will usually list an estimated price, which is the approximate price the seller hopes to get. Your maximum bid should be about 10 percent over the estimated price.

All major auction houses accept bids by mail. You simply send them the maximum price you are willing to pay for an item, and the auctioneer then bids for you as though you were actually there. They are quite reputable and will make sure you get the best price possible, even if it's lower than the amount they know you are willing to spend.

Bidding by mail has the added advantage of helping you avoid "auction fever"—keeping you from getting caught up in the excitement and spending far more than you had intended. If you do attend auctions in person, be sure to set a mental limit before the bidding begins and stick to it.

The auction house is paid a commission by the seller—usually 10 percent of the actual price. Sometimes the buyer is required to pay a commission as well.

## HOW TO SAVE 30 PERCENT OR MORE ON GALLERY PRICES

What if you see something you like in a gallery that you probably won't find at an auction? Remember, the markup on most works of art in galleries can be 30 to 40 percent, and sometimes more. Here's a great way to pay "wholesale": Buy your art through a discount broker! Recently, a subscriber to our newsletter, *Forecasts & Strategies*, saw an Erté bronze sculpture in a gallery. The retail price was a high $12,000. Before buying it, he decided to call Michael Kuschmann, president of Fine Arts, Ltd., our recommended discount broker for artworks. Kuschmann dealt with the gallery directly and got it for cost plus 10 percent. Our subscriber paid only $5,750 for the Erté bronze, a savings of more than 50 percent off retail!

Our advice: Before paying retail for an art piece, contact Fine Arts Ltd., 220 State St., Suite H, Los Altos, CA 94022, or call 800-229-4322 or 415-941-4322. Also obtain a copy of Kuschmann's book, *How To Invest in Art*, for $10. Fine Arts Ltd. specializes in limited edition signed prints of famous artists. You'd be surprised what you can get for under $1,000.

## HOW TO CHOOSE A COLLECTIBLE

Even after you have narrowed the field to a single collectible you could become interested in, you are still faced with having to choose from among hundreds of possible purchases. The following guidelines will help you choose a winner.

• *Stay with quality.* Good pieces hold their value better than items of poor quality; they also sell better at auction. Don't be penny-wise and dollar-foolish when it comes to quality.

• *Look for beauty.* Beautiful objects will always sell well and can give you much aesthetic pleasure over the years if you decide to keep them.

• *Stay away from modern collectibles.* Whether you're investing in stamps, legal tender coins, medallions, paintings or prints, stick with the rare or old item—don't buy newly issued collectibles at high retail prices. You want an object with a proven track record, not something that is likely to sell at below the original price in a few years. Be especially wary of "limited edition" silver ingots, Christmas plates, "rare" books, coins, etc. While a few issues have proven successful, most have not.

• *Look for a ready market.* Don't buy into an exotic field that only a handful of investors are interested in. Stay with the proven collectibles that have plenty of potential buyers around the country and around the world. Also avoid fads—they're too unpredictable for long-term profits.

• *Plan on holding for several years.* When you pay 10 to 15 percent commissions on collectibles, you have to plan on holding them for several years in order to make optimal long-term capital gains.

## BEST BUYS FOR THE SMALL INVESTOR

Let's take a closer look at a few collectible markets that offer the best opportunities for the novice investor who wants fast appreciation on lower-priced items.

### Rare Coins

Rare or numismatic gold and silver coins can still be purchased individually for under $1,000—and even a few for under $300—but most gold coins in both rare and uncirculated condition are much more expensive.

There are three main categories describing the condition of rare coins: proof, brilliant uncirculated and circulated. Proof coins are usually the rarest and consequently the most expensive. They are coins that were set aside for collectors immediately after being struck and have absolutely no blemishes or marks on them. Brilliant uncirculated (BU) coins have never circulated in public either, but they were not set aside and may be scratched with "bag marks" from being carried in mint bags. Circulated coins are also graded, depending on wear and tear.

We recommend the purchase of gold coins in brilliant uncirculated condition—it pays to stay with quality. But the small investor should stay away from proof coins, as they are too rare and consequently too expensive. They also are less in demand and therefore might be difficult to sell. We specifically recommend the $20 Liberty and St. Gauden Double Eagles, the $10 Liberty or Indian Eagles and the $5 Half-Eagles.

The best coins for the beginner may be the rare silver coins because they are generally less expensive than the gold coins. Historically, rare silver coins have outperformed bullion or "junk" silver coins, while minimizing the gut-wrenching drops that occur in the bullion price of silver from time to time.

There are numerous ways to invest in rare silver coins. Some general categories might include:

- Individual Morgan silver dollars, Franklin halves, Washington quarters, Mercury dimes

- Rolls of coins with different dates

- Full-year sets (e.g., 1942 sets of dollars, halves, etc., from each mint)

- Type sets (full sets of Morgan dollars, Franklin halves, etc.)

- Commemorative coins (legal-tender coins issued for a specific anniversary, statehood celebration, special event, etc.)

You can buy rare coins from your local coin dealer, but you'll want to compare prices and quality because prices for the same graded coin can differ substantially among dealers. It's probably best to deal with a large, reliable firm. The following firms specialize in rare coins:

Camino Coins
P.O. Box 4292
Burlingame, CA 94010
800-348-8001

David Hall's
Numismatic Investment
   Group
1936 E. Deere, Suite 102
Santa Anna, Ca 92705
800-359-4255
714-662-3350

Stack's Rare Coins
123 W. 57th St.
New York, NY 10019
212-582-2580

MTB Banking Corp.
30 Rockefeller Plaza
New York, NY 10112
800-535-7481
212-621-9500

Liberty Coin Service
300 Frandor Ave.
Lansing, MI 48912
800-321-1542
517-351-4720

Van Simmons of David Hall's firm is one of the few dealers who continues to buy coins back from customers no matter what the market conditions are. Remember, you need liquidity in every investment and Van Simmons's office offers you just that.

Overgrading and counterfeits have been serious problems from time to time in the rare-coin industry. To avoid these problems, virtually all dealers depend on the grading system developed by the Professional Coin Grading System (PCGS). PCGS grades coins according to a set standard (e.g., MS 60 to MS 70).

The safest place to store your coins is in a safe-deposit box. Be sure to have your coins insured.

Investors should be wary of false advertising claims made by some rare-coin dealers. In the past, some dealers have used the famous Salomon Brothers annual survey of investment performance to promote the idea that rare coins are a "sure deal" investment that has outperformed all other investments over the past ten years. Nothing could be further from the truth. The coins in the Salomon Brothers survey were so rare and unknown that few investors actually bought these coins. A broader index of rare-coin prices indicates that, like all collectibles, rare coins have gone through bull and bear markets and that careful selection is critically important. Salomon Brothers, by the way, eliminated rare coins as a category in 1991 in response to the list's misuse by some rare-coin promoters.

## Postage Stamps

Stamp collecting is the world's leading hobby. Rare stamps, like coins, have a ready market around the world, and the prices of rare stamps have skyrocketed in the past 15 years.

At first, limit your purchase to U.S. stamps that have a proven track record. Avoid the purchase of low-value U.S. commemorative stamps touted by the post office—some sheets are actually worth less than face value to stamp collectors!

Again, stay with high-quality issues, and make sure your stamp collection is well preserved and insured. There are many auction houses in the stamp market, especially in New York City. You'll also find stamp dealers at many coin shows.

## Baseball Cards and Sports Memorabilia

In the 1980s, sports memorabilia became a hot collectible item, beginning with baseball cards. Now collecting autographed sports memorabilia is big business and has spread to football, basketball and hockey.

Still, for the collector, baseball remains America's number-one sport. Old baseball cards of such Hall of Famers as Mickey Mantle, Ted Williams, Willie Mays and Joe DiMaggio were worth pennies when they first came out. Today they are worth hundreds if not thousands of dollars. Mickey Mantle's 1951 rookie card in mint condition recently sold for $50,000, a record. Some suggest that such high prices reflect a tulipmania, however.

If you are going to collect baseball cards, it's best to buy older cards issued prior to 1977. Before then, Topps printed baseball cards in fairly limited numbers, but afterward, collecting cards became a hit and Topps began printing them in much larger quantities. You should also limit your collection to Hall of Famers, or potential Hall of Famers. Buying rookie cards, especially of pitchers, is very risky. Finally, it's best to select mint or near-mint cards.

Collecting baseballs autographed by big-name players is also a reasonable bet. You can get a Mickey Mantle ball for under $100, because he signed so many. But his baseballs will probably increase in value, just as Babe Ruth's have. (The Babe also signed a lot of balls in his lifetime.)

As prices head higher, the investor needs to beware of volatile markets and counterfeiting. In a hot market, speculators often exceed the number of legitimate collectors, and prices can rise sharply and then collapse. Hot markets also encourage counterfeiting of baseball cards, autographed baseballs and other sports memorabilia.

### Rare Books

Rare books can be a rewarding investment, particularly if you enjoy great literature. The quality of the cover and stock, the book's scarcity, the edition and the author's fame are all factors in determining the market value of a rare book.

Certain books in good condition have appreciated steadily in value. Adam Smith's classic, *The Wealth of Nations* (first edition, London 1776), increased in value during the past decade alone from $1,400 to over $25,000—if you can find a copy. Darwin's original *Origin of Species* climbed from $700 in 1970 to over $10,000 today. Other books by famous authors have done equally well.

Nevertheless, because rarity is the most important factor in determining demand, a rare book that sells for $10,000 may appreciate faster and be easier to sell than a $100 book. So, from an investment perspective, if you can afford to invest in genuinely rare books, you should probably avoid lower-priced books that are less in demand.

Auction houses are still the best place to buy and sell rare books. Sotheby's, mentioned earlier, has catalogs on upcoming auctions.

## Autographs

Original manuscripts, letters, directives and other material handwritten by famous people can be valuable to an interested buyer. Autographs vary greatly in price, depending not only on whose it is but also on what it says. Autographs have generally appreciated in price, like all collectibles, but again, watch out for forgeries and avoid the excessive prices charged in galleries or shopping malls. For the best price, go to an auction.

We've watched this growth industry for several years and noted how prices just continue to rise—often much faster than your favorite stock or gold coin. Autographed historical documents have been in a bull market for years, and there seems no end in sight.

The Heritage Collectors' Society offers investment-quality historical documents, signed by famous politicians, scientists, sports figures and military leaders. Recent collections include Ben Franklin, Charles Darwin, Ty Cobb, Charles Dickens, Robert Frost, George Patton, Thomas Jefferson, John F. Kennedy, Franklin D. Roosevelt and Napoleon. The documents are framed for display with a picture of the famous signer. This is one way to enjoy a little bit of history while making a profit.

To obtain the latest catalog, contact Thomas A. Lingenfelter, President, Heritage Collectors' Society, 11 West Court St., Box 2390, Doylestown, PA 18901, 215-345-7955.

## Furniture

Someone who loves history, art and beauty might want to own a desk or armoire that once belonged to a nobleman's family or a porcelain dish that was handcrafted by an artisan. Happily, these items can be good investments as well as objects of beauty.

Many antiques pass through London at some stage in their lives, so prices tend to be lower, and the quality higher, in London than in many other cities. There are antique dealers everywhere in that city, and of every variety, from the Saturday flea market on Portobello Road to the specialized shops in every block of Bond Street to the world-renowned auction houses of Sotheby's and Christie's. Whether you are interested in French writing desks, English porcelain, 19th-century watercolors, Irish crystal, military firearms or your own unusual hobby, you can probably find it in London.

But you don't have to travel to Europe to find antiques. Many fine pieces have already been discovered and imported to the United States, and there are American-made antiques as well. In fact, there are reputable dealers in major cities throughout the country.

When you're ready to do some serious antique hunting, do some research ahead of time. Take a class, go to the library, visit museums, spend time with a restorer and ask questions that reveal your own knowledge so you will be taken seriously.

To help you get started, here are some guidelines:

• Technically, antique furniture is more than 100 years old.
• The value of antique furniture isn't so much in its age or its rarity as in its workmanship.
• Look for evidence of repairs, but don't automatically reject a piece that has been repaired. Antiques are, after all, more than 100 years old and were used as everyday furniture. But be aware that major repairs or replacements, even if skillfully performed, may reduce an antique's value.
• Good restoration makes a good antique. Watch for poorly

matched wood, inconsistent style, clumsy polishing and so on. You can sometimes find real bargains in pieces that need repair, but get a realistic estimate first of how much those repairs will cost. Restoration can be very expensive, especially if you want top-quality results. "Bargains" in extremely bad shape can end up costing more than good pieces.

• Antique furniture can be a good investment, but keep in mind that the piece you buy should suit your purpose at home as well. Visualize a floor plan for your specific rooms before you start buying, and write down actual dimensions. Ask the dealer what kind of arrangements can be made if you find that a piece doesn't fit when you get it home. (Some will buy back, others won't.)

• Buy what pleases you, but also be aware of resale demand. For example, art deco is popular right now, but it might not be ten years from now, while Georgian furniture is always marketable. Fads can affect prices, sometimes drastically, both up and down.

What about fair price? Reputable dealers have fairly standard prices, and numerous books exist with current average prices, such as Kovel's *Antiques and Collectibles Price List* ($9.95, available at your local bookstore).

Auctions can be an exciting way to pick up a bargain—or to get caught in a frenzy of overpayment. It takes a calm exterior and cool self-control, as well as a better-than-average understanding of prices and quality, to do well at an auction. Follow the guidelines we set forth earlier, and consider a trip to Europe's flea markets if you've developed a skilled eye and are interested in making some major purchases.

## FINE ART ON A BUDGET

You can enjoy the beauty of fine art in your home or office, just as the wealthy do, but without paying rare-art prices. Here are two affordable alternatives for the budget-conscious collector:

First, buy limited-edition prints, signed by the artists. Original paintings and drawings by well-known artists often sell for hundreds of thousands of dollars, if not millions. Limited-edition prints are a good alternative. Like the original paintings, the prices of limited-edition prints have been increasing in price. You can obtain works by Renoir, Picasso, Rembrandt, Chagall, Delacroix and McKnight, all for reasonable prices. And, if you buy through the mail, you can save 30 percent or more off the retail gallery price.

For a brochure on the latest mail-order offerings, contact Fine Arts Ltd., 220 State St., Suite H, Los Altos, CA 94022 or call 800-229-4322 or 415-941-4322.

The second alternative is to buy *expert re-creations* of classic art works. For example, you can have a genuine oil painting done by an expert painter re-creating *The Irises* by Van Gogh. For the original painting an investor paid $53 million several years ago, but we paid less than $3,000 for a museum-quality reproduction. Admittedly, these are consumption items, not proven investments, because they have no track record on a secondary market yet, but the primary price continues to rise.

Heritage House Galleries, with offices located in Ft. Lauderdale, Florida, and Carmel, California, offer these unique museum-quality reproductions for reasonable prices. We have several paintings in our own home and enjoy them as much as we would the originals. Perhaps even more, since we would have to keep an original in a vault! You might consider them "legal forgeries." Imagine, having oil paintings designed by Van Gogh, Renoir, Remington and Rembrandt in your home. The price of these re-creations varies with the size and complexity of the painting, but generally prices start at $3,000 and up. Best of all, you aren't limited to choosing from among the paintings hanging in a gallery; you can commission a re-creation of any pre-20th-century painting you happen to like.

For a free brochure, contact Edward A. Mero, Heritage House Galleries, 4800 North State Road 7, Ft. Lauderdale, FL 33319, or call 800-448-4583 or 305-735-5601.

## IN CONCLUSION

There are hundreds of other collectibles available, although some, like classic antique cars, are too expensive, exotic or illiquid for the beginner. Choose something you like for its intrinsic value and learn everything you can about it. Purchase items that are of high quality and that are rare and fairly priced. Become familiar with the major auction houses and be aware of current selling prices. In these days of production-line manufacturing and identical designer clothes and home furnishings, it's nice to know that you can still own a one-of-a-kind collectible. It takes some extra time and research to find that perfect possession, but the results can be extremely rewarding.

As John Marion of Sotheby's states, "Investing in beautiful things is not only a smart way to allocate one's assets, it can also be one of life's great joys. From flea markets, garage sales and antiques shops to big-city galleries and the world's great auction houses, collecting has become America's number-one indoor sport."

# CHAPTER 14

---

# Trading in Futures and Options for the Small Investor

*Now I've a sheep and a cow, everybody bids me good-morrow.*

—Poor Richard's Almanac

THE OPTIONS AND FUTURES markets have expanded tremendously over the past few years. Today there are options on stocks, commodities and even Treasury bonds and currencies. The futures market is expanding just as rapidly. Speculating on the future price of stocks and commodities through options and futures vehicles is undoubtedly the fastest way for the small investor to pyramid a little cache into a large fortune.

When trading commodities, you typically put down only 5 to 10 percent "margin" money, which means you actually control 10 to 20 times the amount of your investment. In options, you can buy a "call" option for a few hundred dollars that will give you the ability to buy several thousand dollars' worth of stock. Real estate may be the only other vehicle that allows you to control significant assets with just a little money down; in real estate, however, you don't have the liquidity you do with options and futures.

## A SHORT COURSE IN OPTIONS TRADING

We introduced the options market in Chapter 10, where we discussed writing call options as a way to increase your income on blue-chip stocks you may hold. Writing call options is probably the lowest-risk approach you can take in this fast-moving market.

In our examples, we saw that the buyer of the call option was speculating that the price of a stock would move up. By purchasing a call option, he was guaranteeing his right to buy 100 shares of the stock at $30 a share. Suppose the call option cost $350, including commissions. Now, let's suppose also that the stock rises to $50 a share, and the speculator exercises the option to buy it at $30 a share. His paper profit is $2,000 on an investment of $350. If he had bought the stock outright, he would have made a 67 percent profit, but by buying an option, he made nearly 500 percent profit!

What are the risks of buying call options? For one thing, if the price of the stock declines, the buyer doesn't exercise his option and it expires worthless, his $350 wasted. Fortunately, he cannot lose more than his original investment (unlike commodities futures, as we shall see), but he can lose all of that money. In fact, the speculator will also lose his total $350 investment if the price of the stock stays the same during the life of the option contract, because the option will expire unexercised and worthless at the end of its designated life span.

Because options expire in a short period of time, the key to profits is short-term forecasting. This is extremely difficult to do. Time works against the option buyer. As a result, studies indicate that 80 percent of all options buyers lose money. Does this mean that selling options rather than buying them could be more profitable?

Many speculators make consistent profits by selling options, but there is high risk here, too, if you don't actually own the stock on which you sell the option. If you feel certain that the price of a particular stock will drop, you might sell an option for that stock even though you don't own it, expecting the contract to expire unexercised. You then pocket the money. This is called selling *naked* calls, and it can be extremely dangerous, because if the price of the stock goes up, you are required to deliver the stock at the strike price (in our example, $30 for the stock), and if you don't own the stock, you have to buy it on the open market. Suppose that stock rises to $50 a share. You have to buy it at $50 and sell it at $30—losing $20 a share. As you can see, your losses could conceivably be unlimited because the price of the stock could rise to any level.

## Puts and Calls on Stock Indices

One of the most exciting developments in recent years has been the creation of put and call options on stock market indices. Trading the *OEX*, as it is called, is a way for any investor—large or small—to profit from movements in the whole stock market, whether up or down. The OEX is traded on the Chicago Board of Trade and stands for options on the S&P 100 stock futures index.

Here's how it works: Suppose you think the stock market is headed higher. You tell your broker to buy a call option on the OEX. You need to decide the date of the option (when it will expire) and the exercise price (also called the strike price). Suppose you buy a call that expires in June and the exercise price is 400. The cost of this option is $200. Suppose, also, that the S&P 100 is at 390 currently. Buying a call option gives you the right to buy the S&P 100 stock futures index, which is worth $39,000. You only had to pay $200 for this right to control $39,000 worth of stock. Now, that's leverage!

Let's assume that in the next month, the stock market rallies and the S&P 100 stock index rises to 420. That means the S&P 100 futures contract is now worth $42,000. If you exercised the call option, you'd pay $40,000 for the contract (100 shares × the 400 exercise price), and could then resell it for $42,000. Your profit would be $2,000. You made ten times your money based on the initial $200 investment!

Suppose, however, that you were wrong and the stock market went nowhere, or declined in value. You'd lose your $200, and no more.

You can also make money when the market declines by buying a put option on the OEX. It works the same way, but in reverse.

In sum, playing the OEX is a great way for the small investor to get rich quick, with limited downside potential. But remember, you can lose two ways: (1) if the market goes against you and (2) if your timing is off. In order to make money buying options, timing must be on your side.

As a small speculator, you can play the options game if you meet the minimum investment and income requirements. But we don't recommend it unless you have at least several thousand dollars in cash and are pretty confident about what you are doing.

A discount brokerage firm that assists small speculators in the options market is:

Marquette de Bary Co.
488 Madison Ave.
New York, NY 10022
800-221-3305
212-644-5300

## THE BASICS OF COMMODITY FUTURES

Many people think that the futures market is just a form of gambling, but it has a legitimate business function. The futures markets began as a way to allow farmers, ranchers and other commodity producers to hedge themselves against rising costs. To be more specific, a cattle rancher's profits are based not only on the price he gets for his cattle, but on the amount it costs him to raise that cattle. If a drought or blight destroys half the corn crop, it could double the rancher's feed bill.

Since there is no way to predict the price of feed with certainty, a rancher will lock in the current price for feed, signing a *forward* or *futures* contract to purchase a certain number of bushels at a fixed price within a specified time. If prices do indeed rise, the farmer who sold the futures contract must still provide the specified amount of feed to the rancher at the lower price. Of course, if bumper crops drive the price of feed lower, the rancher must still purchase the agreed-on feed at the agreed-on (higher) price.

On one hand, the rancher has limited his profits potential, but on the other hand, he has limited his risk.

Business people who deal in foreign trade also use the futures market to hedge against uncertainty. For example, an importer of Japanese calculators will buy futures contracts on the Japanese yen so that he knows exactly how much his foreign exchange costs will be; if the dollar weakens and the yen skyrockets, his import costs will not go up.

As you can see, for the producer who must rely on large commodity purchases for his business, the futures market is actually a conservative investment, a way to protect himself from future price rises.

## How To Play the Futures Market

Suppose your investor's instincts tell you that the price of a specific commodity, platinum perhaps, is going to increase. You could buy the metal at the current price—let's say $400—and take delivery of it (either physical possession or in the form of a warehouse receipt) and then resell it when (if) the price goes up. You would have to come up with the full amount, or buy on margin and pay interest on the unpaid balance. In addition, you would pay commissions both to buy and to sell.

Instead, you could opt to buy a platinum contract on the futures market. You could purchase a platinum contract for January of next year selling for, say, $405. You have not actually bought the platinum yet; this contract simply gives you the opportunity to buy platinum at $405 any time before January. For this guarantee you will pay a commission and place a good-faith deposit of 5 to 10 percent of the total cash price.

Now you play a waiting game. Suppose the current price of platinum reaches $450 in September. You could exercise your contract, buying the metal for $405, and immediately sell it for $450, gaining $45 per ounce, or $4,500 for the contract. But since you have only had to come up with 10 percent, or $405 for the contract (plus a little more for commissions), your actual profit is more than 10 times your investment!

Of course, this is the ideal scenario. Your actual experience is likely to be quite different. Greed can get the better of you. You might not exercise the contract in September, thinking the metal is headed even higher, only to find later that September's price was the top. Worse, the price of platinum could fall instead of rise, and you might lose your entire investment.

### Selling Short

The above example is called *buying long*, and it's fairly straightforward: You buy a commodity and then resell it. It's called *buying long* regardless of the time that lapses in between. *Selling short* requires you to sell something before you actually have it. With a short contract, you are agreeing to sell a specific commodity at a specific price within a specific time. The catch, of course, is that you will have to purchase or produce that commodity at some time in order to fulfill the contract. In a way, you are acting as a supplier or middleman, although the commodity never actually goes through your hands.

Suppose you expect the price of cocoa to drop in the future, perhaps because of bumper crops or reduced demand. You agree to sell cocoa in December for, let's say, $2,100 per ton, the price on the futures market for December cocoa. Sure enough, in July the price of cocoa drops to $1,800. You buy the cocoa for $1,800 and sell it (to an investor who owns a long contract) for $2,100 at the contract price, pocketing the difference.

You don't even have to wait until December to take your profits, since you can "cover your position" by purchasing a long contract in cocoa, in essence promising to buy and sell to yourself. Again, because you only had to pay a small percentage of the actual contract price, if you make a profit, it can exceed 100 percent.

Keep in mind, though, that if you predict incorrectly, you could end up having to buy cocoa for $2,500 and sell it for $2,100, thereby taking a substantial loss. In fact, selling short is much riskier than buying long, because in selling short your losses are unlimited. The most a commodity can drop to is zero, but it can rise to any price, and if you are selling short, you would still have to fulfill the contract.

Many investment experts have developed elaborate trading programs and strategies to try to predict the commodities markets. One popular strategy is the "production cost" theory. This plan is based on the theory that if a commodity's price drops below its production cost (that is, the amount it costs to grow or mine it), the price will absolutely have to go back up, and soon.

But new technology often reduces production costs, and substitute products can reduce demand. The moral of this story is that nothing is a sure thing.

In an inflationary climate, rising prices are the natural expectation and buying long is the most reasonable response, but despite continued inflation, the commodity market went through a major bear market in the past decade.

Because of the huge risks involved, brokerage firms require evidence of substantial net worth before they will accept your purchase order, to make sure you can afford margin calls and complete losses. A net worth of $200,000, excluding real estate holdings, and an income of $50,000 are not unusual requirements.

## FOUR STEPS TO LOW-RISK TRADING

Clearly, then, commodity trading can be a highly lucrative but risky business. Fortunately, there are ways to reduce your risks, even though you can't eliminate them. Let us emphasize four important points.

First, look for commodities that are in a "sideways" pattern. When you look at the commodities charts, you will find that some commodities have maintained a fairly constant price for a period of time—their graphs move sideways, or horizontally. Place a buy order 5 or 10 percent above the current price, and wait for the price to move out of the sideways pattern. (Or, if you think the price will break downward, you could place a sell order and wait for the price to drop.)

The advantage to this approach is that you won't enter a commodity market until the price comes to you, so that the trend will already have begun before you buy. But you will be close enough to the beginning of the trend to take full advantage of it. Another advantage to this method is that while your money isn't tied up in trading, it can earn interest in a money market fund or in Treasury bills.

Second, place a *stop-loss* order as the price moves up. A stop-loss order is an order to your broker to sell when the market declines to a certain price. If the price is never reached, the order is never filled. *Trailing stops* are stop-loss orders that you adjust to follow the rise (or fall, if you're selling short) of the price of the commodity. Trailing stop-loss orders are essential to preserving your profits. They should be flexible enough to allow for small corrections so that you're not stopped out too early, but tight enough to get you out of the market before the bottom drops out. A good rule of thumb is to place stop-loss orders 10 to 15 percent away from the current price. As profits become more substantial, you can afford to widen your profit margin.

Third, pyramid conservatively. Pyramiding is a way to multiply your profits even further. As the price of a commodity moves up and you make more money, your account will show growing equity on paper. For example, if wheat increases in price from $5 to $6, your "paper profits" are $1,000 on a 1,000-bushel contract. You can then use that $1,000 to buy additional contracts.

There's a right way and a wrong way to pyramid, as shown in Figure 14.1. The right way is to add fewer contracts as the price climbs. If you start out with three contracts in wheat, you could conservatively add one or two contracts as the price moves up. The wrong way is to add five or six contracts—more than what you started with. Why? Because if the price suddenly reverses, you could lose all of your profits quickly.

**Figure 14.1**
Pyramiding

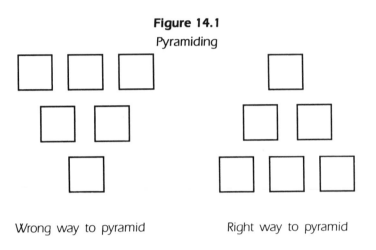

Wrong way to pyramid          Right way to pyramid

Fourth, never buy or sell a contract on a hot tip or a hunch. Be rational, study your charts and the fundamental economic factors and read the financial newspapers. Most important, be your own money manager. Listen to your broker's theories if you want, but make your own decisions, and use your broker only for executing those decisions.

## MIDAMERICA EXCHANGE: SMALL SPECULATOR'S DELIGHT

The major commodity exchanges—such as the Chicago Board of Trade (CBOT), the New York Mercantile Exchange and the International Monetary Exchange—allow you to trade in a variety of commodities, including agricultural commodities, metals and financial instruments. They require a fairly substantial minimum investment, which prevents most average earners from getting into the futures market.

However, the MidAmerica Commodity Exchange in Chicago, which was bought by the Chicago Board of Trade, offers a unique alternative for the beginner. It provides for very small contracts in several commodities—cattle, hogs, soybeans, corn, oats, wheat, silver and gold, as well as foreign currencies and U.S. Treasury securities. The main advantage is MidAmerica's lower minimums. For example, while the Chicago Board of Trade has a minimum wheat contract of 5,000 bushels, MidAmerica allows a 1,000-bushel contract. The initial margin requirement on CBOT wheat is about $1,500, while MidAmerica's margin is only $300. Table 14.1 demonstrates the advantages more specifically.

Under these conditions, it's possible for the small trader to start speculating with $1,000. Of course, he must have additional funds to back up his margin requirements in case of a margin call.

### Table 14.1
### MidAmerica's Contract Sizes

| Commodity | Size of Contract | | Initial Margin | |
|---|---|---|---|---|
| | Major Exchange | Mid-America | Major Exchange | Mid-America |
| Cattle | 40,000 lbs. | 20,000 lbs. | $ 1,500 | $400 |
| Corn | 5,000 bu. | 1,000 bu. | $ 1,000 | $100 |
| N.Y. silver | 5,000 oz. | 1,000 oz. | $20,000 | $300 |
| N.Y. gold | 100 oz. | 33.2 oz. | $ 9,000 | $465 |

A study by the Commodity Futures Trading Commission showed that more than 62 percent of commodity traders had less than $5,000 in their accounts. That would be enough for only a couple of contracts on the big boards. But, with MidAmerica, you could take several positions, make more trades and limit your dollar commitment. Risk is a major concern in commodity trading, and minicontracts spread that risk.

For a booklet on the MidAmerica exchange, write or call:

    The MidAmerica Commodity Exchange
    141 West Jackson Blvd.
    Chicago, IL 60604
    312-341-3000

Once you get a better handle on commodities by trading the minicontracts on MidAmerica, you might try your hand at contracts in commodities at larger exchanges.


## CHOOSING A DISCOUNT COMMODITY BROKER

A good commodity broker, like a good stockbroker, is hard to find. You won't find many who are willing to let you trade your own way, and they are especially impatient with the waiting game of trading sideways patterns.

Commodity brokers are paid a set commission per commodity contract. Sometimes brokers from major firms set their own commission rates, so see if yours is willing to negotiate.

Discounters have entered the commodity markets, although they are far less numerous than stock market discount houses. There are risks entailed in using a discount commodity broker, however. A securities account is insured, but a commodity account is not. Recently some commodity houses have gone bankrupt, leaving many traders holding an empty bag. Be sure to check out the financial soundness of a discount broker before committing funds.

Here are several discount commodity brokers you may wish to consider:

| | |
|---|---|
| First American | Futures Discount Group |
| 800-621-4415 | 800-872-6673 |
| 312-368-4700 | 312-444-1155 |

Ira Epstein & Co.
800-284-6000
312-407-5700

Jack Carl
800-621-3424
312-407-5700

TransMarket Group
800-362-8117
312-663-4972

## MANAGED COMMODITY ACCOUNTS

One other low-budget alternative for the individual speculator is to invest in a managed commodity plan. While the minimum investment for individually managed accounts is $25,000 and sometimes higher at large brokerage firms, pooled "mutual funds" in commodities typically have a $5,000 minimum. These plans offer the professional management of trading experts, as well as diversification and spreading of risk because the money of numerous investors is pooled. The risks are significant, though, because professional management does not guarantee profits. Many funds have performed extremely well, gaining over 100 percent a year, and then have suddenly lost money.

Moreover, managed accounts are notorious for charging high management fees and commissions. So, when you consider a managed account, examine the full costs of the plan—they can be substantial.

Recently several commodity funds have been created to reduce the costs of trading and minimize the risks. Two examples:

• *Shearson Futures 1000-Plus series of commodity funds*, issued from time to time by Shearson Lehman Brothers. The fund guarantees the return of principal after five years, no matter how poorly the futures portion has traded. They do this by putting 65 percent of the initial capital into zero-coupon bonds that mature at face value within five years. The remaining 35 percent is invested in the commodity market by a trading expert. The costs of a commodity fund include commissions, management fees, overhead and other costs, and they can be considerable. The average cost of a commodity fund is over 20 percent a year, but Shearson's funds average an annual cost of under 13 percent. For more information, contact Shearson Lehman Brothers in your area.

• *Alternative Asset Growth Fund*, a limited partnership designed by ProFutures, Inc., in Austin, Texas. ProFutures selects the top five commodity managers and divides the fund's assets among them. The fund is diversified into all commodity categories. You are guaranteed no margin calls, and you can withdraw your funds at the end of any month. ProFutures seeks to keep the annual cost of each fund at approximately 8 percent. For more information, contact ProFutures, Inc., 107 Hwy. 620 South, Suite 30F, Austin, TX 78734, 800-348-3601 or 512-263-3800.

One newsletter that monitors managed commodity accounts is *Managed Account Reports*, 5513 Twin Knolls Rd., Suite 213, Columbia, MD 21045, $225 a year.

## A FINAL WORD

Options and futures trading are not for everyone, but by following the guidelines set out in this chapter, you can greatly reduce the risks. Big profits are available, but it takes a strong stomach and patient fortitude to realize them. Most important, use only your speculative funds for options and futures, while maintaining your conservative investments as a solid foundation.

# CHAPTER 15

# Invest in Yourself: The Reward of a Small Business

*Keep thy shop, and thy shop will keep thee.*

—Poor Richard's Almanac

EVERY YEAR, *FORBES* MAGAZINE publishes a list of the 400 richest people in America. What would you say is the most common source of their wealth? Real estate? Oil? The stock market? Surprisingly, it's none of these. The most common source of wealth is their own business! Consequently, when you begin thinking about how you are going to achieve financial independence, it may be best to start thinking about your full-time work first, rather than trying to make big money in stocks, commodities or real estate.

The advantages of having your own business are many. Through careful planning, you can defer taxes on your earnings—almost indefinitely. When you do finally pay taxes, it's at low, favorable rates. There are no minimums, maximums or margin calls. You can pyramid your profits with very little risk. And you can earn money doing something you really enjoy.

Investing in yourself can be a source of great personal satisfaction, as well as a source of profits. Money is a great reward for having chosen wise investments, but it can't match the joy that comes from knowing you are a success in your own business.

In today's uncertain world, it pays to learn a second trade or job skill. The economy is on a roller-coaster ride, and no one's job is absolutely secure. Consequently, it's extremely important that you not only establish an investment program but seek out new business opportunities.

## THE OUTLOOK FOR SMALL BUSINESS

There are numerous business opportunities that don't require a lot of money up front. Since this is something that will involve a lot more of your time than will most investments, make sure you choose something you like, and not just something with the highest profit potential.

Consider the opportunities available today.

• *Learn a new skill.* There will always be a heavy demand for competent artisans and repairmen in almost every field. Learning to build cabinets, repair plumbing, upholster furniture, fix cars, photograph children or type legal drafts can provide a sizeable second income and give you a tangible insurance policy against bad times.

• *Sell unique information.* Everyone has specialized knowledge of some sort, whether it's a unique recipe, a new way to make money, a way to improve office efficiency or a better way to raise children. Packaging this information can take many forms—cassette tapes, books, newsletters, seminars and television programming are just a few. The mail-order business, in particular, can provide an easy way to get started fast with little capital investment. Many shrewd entrepreneurs with a marketable idea have started with just a $50 ad in the classifieds section of a newspaper or magazine, and turned it into thousands of dollars in a surprisingly short time.

• *Become a salesperson.* Selling cosmetics, encyclopedias, cleaning products or vitamins to your friends or neighbors may seem pedestrian to some, but if you have the personality for sales, it may be just right for you. It is highly competitive, and high volume is essential to success. Some people are born salesmen, and if you have an easy way of talking with people, a creative flair for advertising, a way of judging other people's needs and a product you honestly believe in, you may be able to join the hundreds of men and women who have become millionaires through direct sales.

• *Become a broker.* As more people enter the stock market for the first time, business is booming in the major brokerage houses, where stocks, bonds, mutual funds, coins, collectibles, insurance and other investments are bought and sold. Most brokerage firms offer their own educational facilities for beginning employees and for those who want to work part-time.

• *Become a consultant.* This is another fast-growing area that deserves looking into, particularly for those who have chosen early retirement. If you've had a distinguished career in government service or achieved success in a large corporation, you may have special inside knowledge that other companies desperately need and are willing to pay big money for. Several courses advertised in *The Wall Street Journal* and other business publications tell you how to become a profitable consultant.

## FRANCHISES: LOW-RISK, HIGH-RETURN OPPORTUNITY

Another popular alternative is to buy a franchise, no matter what your age or income level. You don't have to have a six-figure bank account to buy a franchise. Best of all, government figures show that while 65 percent of all new businesses fail within the first five years, only 5 percent of franchises have failed since 1971—a favorable statistic.

About 1,900 companies offer franchises nationwide, from the big conglomerates like Burger King and Holiday Inn to the smaller service companies like Merry Maid, Diet Center and

Yo-Pop. Initial costs—for the franchise fee, office setup, inventory and the like—can be as little as $15,000, or as much as $2 million.

There are several reasons why buying a franchise rather than starting a business can increase your chances of success.

- You will have instant product recognition. Although your business is brand-new, the product will have a track record.
- You will have national advertising developed by professional ad agencies, an edge that few new businesses can afford.
- You will be able to use carefully developed management and bookkeeping techniques.
- You will have a parent organization to help with any legal problems, a significant consideration in today's lawsuit-happy society. The parent company can also help with obtaining credit through channels that are often closed to untested businesses.
- You will know your investment's costs from the outset.

Of course, there are risks and drawbacks to any business. First, the advantages of product recognition and national advertising come at a cost. In addition to the initial franchise purchase price, you will be expected to pay royalty and advertising fees. These vary from company to company and can be a percentage of gross or a flat fee per customer. Discuss this cost with other franchise owners before signing up.

Second, your creativity may be limited because even though you technically own the store, the franchiser owns the trademark. Therefore, you're prevented from making what you may deem to be necessary changes if they're not approved by the holder of the trademark. For example, McDonald's operators were prevented from offering tomatoes on their hamburgers for years because Ray Kroc, the company founder, didn't allow them.

Third, as with any business, location and management are critical. Make sure the franchise guarantees you a territory. Many franchisers make no such promises, and you could find yourself in head-to-head competition with an identical business.

Fourth, there is an unfortunate lack of concrete information about profits. Franchisers are prohibited by law from telling potential franchise owners their potential profits because the regulators fear that franchisers will mislead potential purchasers if they're allowed to give such information. Consequently, you must do your own research, particularly by studying financial and legal disclosures and by talking with current franchisees.

For more information on franchises, contact the International Franchise Association, 1350 New York Ave., N.W., Suite 900, Washington, D.C. 20005, 202-628-8000.

## WHERE TO FIND START-UP CAPITAL

When we were first married, we soon realized that we would never get wealthy working for someone else. We both craved the freedom to work, write and produce on our own schedules and at our own pace. Mail order seemed like a good way to get started. We began by using our own savings to manufacture a product and advertise it for sale in magazines. We started small, using our savings but avoiding debt. As orders came in, we reinvested all of our profits to expand our advertising and increase our inventories. Within five years we were working 16-hour days just to fill all the orders. Within ten years, we had retired from the mail-order business and become full-time writers, with the freedom to travel, to work at our own pace—and to invest in other people's businesses.

Investing in yourself can be the most profitable vehicle you will ever find, but it is not necessarily wise to put all of your funds into a new business as we did. The wealthy bankroll themselves with "OPM"—Other People's Money—and perhaps you should, too. You could use OPM indirectly, by seeking a business loan from a bank, but this can be costly in terms of interest and difficult in terms of qualifying. Banks want to see collateral and a track record before lending to small businesses. New businesses often have neither.

Instead, you may want to seek a backer. You run the business, and the backer provides the start-up capital for a percentage of the profits and/or ownership. Some may object to the idea of doing all the work of running the business while someone else sits back and takes 15 to 25 percent of the profits, but remember that without the start-up capital, there would be no business. Seventy-five percent of something is better than 100 percent of nothing! A big advantage to partnership over a simple collateralized loan is that the money partner takes all the financial risk. If the business fails, you do not have to repay the money that was invested.

Many wealthy investors actively seek the lucrative profit potential of investing in someone else's business. These venture capitalists advertise in the classifieds section of newspapers and attend conferences and seminars aimed at the small entrepreneur. Word-of-mouth networking is another way to find venture capital. Contact wealthy friends or acquaintances and present them with your business idea. When you are ready to make your pitch, be well prepared. Demonstrate your specific knowledge and skill in the area, present accurate figures regarding costs and potential demand, and convince the backer of your willingness to work hard at making this business a success. The backer will have a legal contract drawn up, and you should hire a separate attorney to go over it for you.

## FOR MORE INFORMATION

Many books and articles have been written on the subject of starting your own business. If you are looking for a backer, or if you are considering investing in someone else's new venture yourself, you should also try to get a copy of Arthur Lipper's book *Venture's Guide to Investing in Private Companies*. The book is now out of print, but you may be able to find it in your library or local trade bookstore. Lipper has had years of experience in raising capital for new businesses, and his book is complete.

James R. Cook's book, *Start-Up Entrepreneur* (New American Library, 120 Woodbine St., Bergenfield, NJ 07621, $14.95), is also very helpful for those who are setting up a new business or who already own a business.

## ONE FINAL WARNING

Make sure you test the market before spending a lot of money on your part-time business. Choose a business that doesn't require a great deal of capital investment at first. Then, once your business is established, you can expand and invest more.

You can lose big money speculating in the investment field, but you can lose it just as fast in new ventures. Remember that there are two potential reasons why no one else is selling your idea or product: Either they haven't thought of it yet, in which case you're in luck, or they know it isn't a very good idea, in which case you could fail. It takes careful test-marketing to know the difference. Good luck!

# CHAPTER 16

---

# Keep What You Earn— Are Tax Shelters for You?

*The hardest thing in the world to understand is the income tax.*

—ALBERT EINSTEIN

As THE AMOUNT WE pay for federal, state and local taxes increases, aggressive tax planning plays an increasing role in the financial lives of more and more Americans. Taxes are on the minds of everyone today, not just the rich. Soon all Americans will be searching for loopholes with which to beat the tax man.

In 1986, Congress passed legislation that reduced the number of tax brackets for individual taxpayers but also eliminated a number of popular deductions while sharply increasing corporate taxes.

What's important to keep in mind is that the new tax brackets apply to taxable income, after you allow for personal exemptions, deductions and credits. Consequently, you could have a gross salary of $40,000 but be in the 15 percent bracket if your total deductions equal $15,000, thereby making your taxable income $25,000. This illustrates that it pays to reduce your taxable income by maximizing your deductions.

Here are some ways you can increase your deductions and reduce your taxable income.

## TAXES AND YOUR OWN HOME

Owning your own home offers many tax advantages, in addition to the possibility of price appreciation. Interest on your mortgage is tax deductible. You can also sell your house, buy a new one within two years and postpone the capital gains tax on any price appreciation you may have realized. After age 55, you can sell your home without purchasing a new one and pocket up to $125,000 in profits completely free of federal income tax.

Buying rental properties used to be the premier tax shelter for the average investor, but the 1986 legislation sharply reduced the tax advantages of investing in income-producing properties. Now the best you can do is offset passive income (interest, dividends, rents) with depreciation and interest deductions. Unless you qualify as a full-time real estate investor, you can no longer deduct your negative cash flow against earned income from your salary. The working woman living mainly on salary can no longer reduce her tax burden to zero with real estate losses.

## INDIVIDUAL RETIREMENT ACCOUNTS AND COMPANY PENSION PLANS

One of the most popular tax shelters for low- and middle-income earners is the Individual Retirement Account (IRA). The government left the IRA deduction intact for many middle-class taxpayers. Unfortunately, though, the deduction is phased out for single individuals earning more than $25,000 and for married couples earning more than $40,000.

If you qualify for an IRA, you can deduct up to $2,000 in contributions from your taxable income, subject to certain income limitations, and all dividends, interest and capital gains earned within the IRA are tax-deferred until you withdraw your retirement funds at age 59½ or later. Instead of paying one-third of your investment earnings to the government each year, your total investment continues to compound returns for you.

But don't forget the disadvantages: If you withdraw the money before age 59½, it is subject to a 10 percent penalty, plus current taxes, and the money you withdraw at retirement is taxed at ordinary income rates. No one knows for sure what those rates will be by the time you retire—they could be higher or lower than the current rates, but we suspect they'll be higher. Still, it is anticipated that your income will be lower at retirement, pushing you into a lower tax bracket. Thus, even though overall rates may be higher when you retire, your personal rate is likely to be lower than it is during your peak earning years.

If you do open an IRA, make sure it is a self-directed plan. Avoid bank plans that restrict your funds to low-return certificates of deposit that hardly keep up with the cost of living. Consider individual retirement plans offered by large brokerage firms, such as Merrill Lynch, Dean Witter, Prudential Securities, etc. For a small administrative fee, they allow you to invest in stocks, bonds and mutual funds (but watch out for high commissions on the "load" mutual funds).

You can also establish an IRA with any of the families of mutual funds listed in Chapter 8. Mutual fund families offer an incredible array of funds specializing in stocks, bonds, gold, foreign stocks and money market accounts, among others. The fees are minimal, and you can switch from one fund to another by using their toll-free number.

Charles Schwab & Co., the nation's largest discount brokerage firm, has an excellent IRA plan, which includes more than 150 no-load mutual funds. In our opinion, Schwab offers the most flexible plan, because it allows you to switch among no-load mutual funds just by making a toll-free telephone call; to switch funds on your own would require a great deal of time and paperwork. Schwab also charges no annual fee for IRA holders. For details, write or call a local office or:

Charles Schwab & Co.
101 Montgomery St.
San Francisco, CA 94104
800-648-5300
415-627-7000

Company pension plans also offer ways to defer taxes. Self-employed persons can set up a self-directed pension plan, contributing up to $30,000 a year, or 20 percent of income. The tax advantages are basically the same whether you are incorporated or a single proprietorship. The best type of company pension program is a "defined benefit" plan, which, in many cases, allows you to contribute more than $30,000 a year. Establish yourself as the trustee of the plan so that you can make your own investment decisions. Major brokerage firms and mutual fund families have brochures on setting up defined-benefit pension plans.

If you work for someone else, your employer may offer one of several popular alternatives, such as a 401(k) and profit-sharing plans. If you have questions, check with the company officer in charge of the program.

## THE ADVANTAGES OF INCORPORATING

The small businessperson may wish to incorporate, for a variety of reasons. Incorporating is often called the "ultimate tax shelter." Federal corporate tax rates are actually better than individual rates, except at the highest income level, as shown in Table 16.1.

**Table 16.1**
Federal Corporate Income Tax Rates

| Taxable Income | Tax Rate |
| --- | --- |
| Up to $50,000 | 15% |
| $50,000–$75,000 | 25% |
| $76,000–$100,000 | 34% |
| $101,000–$335,000 | 39% |

Corporations pay only 15 percent in federal taxes on profits up to $50,000. Compare this to the individual rate, which reaches 28 percent on earnings of just $17,900 for single individuals and $35,800 for married joint filers. The tax advantage disappears, however, for high-income corporations. The corporate rate eventually rises to 39 percent, higher than the 31 percent maximum rate for individuals. Nevertheless, the tax advantages of incorporating are superior for small and growing businesses. Of course there are additional fees, and more government paperwork to consider, but most self-employed individuals can usually save taxes by incorporating.

One of the least expensive ways to incorporate is to use Ted Nicholas's book *How To Form Your Own Corporation Without a Lawyer for Under $75.* To order, send $25 to Enterprise • Dearborn, 520 N. Dearborn St., Chicago, IL 60610. Nicholas has been helping people set up corporations for years.

## VARIABLE ANNUITIES

The insurance industry has developed one of the best ways for investors to defer taxes on their investment funds. It's called the variable annuity, the most exciting tax-free investment vehicle to come along in years. Here's how it works:

Suppose you have $10,000 to invest, and you are considering a $10,000 variable annuity. What are the benefits?

Variable annuities give you the opportunity to invest in several specialized funds in stocks, bonds, foreign investments and natural resources. You can earn interest, dividends and capital gains without paying current taxes. You can switch among funds without penalty or taxes. They are excellent tax-deferral vehicles for investors.

Two variable annuities with low costs and flexible plans are:

• *Vanguard's Variable Annuity.* Annual fees for insurance and administration are only 1 percent. It has no up-front load or early-withdrawal penalties. Four funds are available. Minimum investment is $5,000. Contact Vanguard, P.O. Box 2600, Valley Forge, PA 19482, 800-522-5555.

• *Scudder Horizon Plan.* Annual fees are 1.5 percent, but Scudder offers seven fund choices, including its international fund. Contact Scudder, 160 Federal St., Boston, MA 02110, 800-225-2470.

For more information on variable annuities and other insurance products, contact:

David T. Phillips & Co.
Independent Insurance
   Brokers
3200 N. Dobson Rd.,
   Bldg. C
Chandler, AZ 85224
800-223-9610
602-897-6088

Western Capital
   Financial Group
1925 Century Park East,
   Suite 2350
Los Angeles, CA 90067
800-423-4891
310-556-5499

## TAX-FREE MUNICIPAL BONDS

The well-to-do buy municipal bonds (munis) because they are free from federal taxes and, in some cases, from state and local taxes as well. If you're in the 28 percent tax bracket, a 5 percent return from munis is as good as a return of nearly 8 percent on taxable investments such as corporate bonds, money market funds and stocks.

Municipal bonds are issued in denominations of $5,000, which is another reason why only the well-to-do buy them. Now, however, through municipal bond funds, you can invest in munis with as little as $1,000. Consider the municipal bond funds on page 196.

Vanguard has the widest variety of municipal bond funds, from a money market portfolio to a high-yield portfolio, based on the average length of maturity for the bonds. The longer the maturity, the higher the monthly return. The highest-return funds are also the riskiest. If interest rates rise, the value of the long-term municipal bond fund can drop sharply.

| Fund | Minimum | Writing Privilege? |
|---|---|---|
| Fidelity Tax-Free High Yield<br>Devonshire St.<br>Boston, MA 02109<br>800-544-6666 | $2,500 | Yes |
| Scudder Managed Municipal Bonds<br>160 Federal St.<br>Boston, MA 02110<br>800-225-2470 | $1,000 | No |
| SteinRoe Tax-Exempt Bond Fund<br>P.O. Box 1131<br>Chicago, IL 60690<br>800-338-2550 | $2,500 | Yes |
| Vanguard Muni Bond-High Yield<br>Valley Forge, PA 19482<br>800-662-7447 | $3,000 | Yes |

## TAX SHELTERS IN LIMITED PARTNERSHIPS

Exotic tax shelters have traditionally been the exclusive domain of the rich. Tax shelters could include investments in limited partnerships in real estate, oil and gas drilling, movies, gold mines, equipment leasing, etc. In the 1970s and 1980s, such partnerships offered incredible write-offs, sometimes two or three times the original investment or more.

Major brokerage firms still offer limited partnerships in oil and gas, real estate and low-income housing, to name just a few. But the game has changed as tax rates have been reduced and "loopholes" have been closed or tightened. The minimum investment is typically $5,000, but the current-year write-offs have been sharply reduced. If you are interested in the latest partnership offerings, contact a well-known brokerage firm in your area.

A few public limited partnerships trade on the major stock

exchanges. In oil, they include Samson, Sun, and Diamond Shamrock; in real estate, they include Burger King (which owns the land and buildings where Burger Kings operate) and Red Lion. These public partnerships pay annual cash distributions that are often partially tax-deferred. They do not offer up-front deductions, however. The minimum investment is typically $10 to $15 a share, as opposed to $2,000 to $5,000 for a limited partnership through a broker.

## DEALING WITH THE IRS

Your tax worries are not finished when you file your tax return. There is still the possibility of an audit to consider.

Only a small percentage of individuals are audited by the IRS each year, but the chances increase as your salary and the complexity of your return increase.

It may be a good idea to get help when you prepare your tax return. It may keep you from overpaying (a recent study showed that 80 percent of American taxpayers pay more tax than necessary), as well as reduce the chances of an audit. It is also helpful to include photocopies of your documents verifying deductions that may otherwise cause the IRS computer to "kick out" your return for further scrutiny and possible audit. For example, if you are a full tithe-payer to your church, you are paying more than the national norm, and the computer is likely to flag your return. If you have attached copies of your contribution receipts, however, the auditor will be likely to okay your return without a full-scale audit.

If you are audited, it's usually best to have representation by an accountant or attorney, whether your return was prepared by them or not.

There are several books on the market today dealing with this subject, but we feel the best one is *How To Do Business with the IRS* by Randy Bruce Blaustein (Prentice-Hall Press, Englewood Cliffs, NJ 07632).

## SUMMARY OF TAX SHELTERS

Tax shelters aren't necessary for every investor, but as you become more successful in your business or profession and your income increases, tax-deferred techniques make more and more sense. Tax shelters in pension plans, real estate, insurance plans and limited partnerships will prove extremely valuable, but keep in mind that in every case, it's imperative that you investigate the financial soundness of an investment first to make sure it will make money and not just reduce your taxes.

# CHAPTER 17

# Your Investment Portfolio from $100 to $10,000

*The great thing in this world is not so much where we stand as in what direction we are moving.*

—OLIVER WENDELL HOLMES

Now WE COME TO an important question: What kind of investments are suitable at different levels of income and net worth?

We created the $100 investment portfolio in 1981 to prove a point: today the world of high finance is available to all investors, not just to the rich.

While the $100 investment portfolio is suitable for all investors at any level of income, it is fairly conservative and emphasizes steady, long-term gains.

Many investors, of course, want more out of their investment program, so we've also developed alternatives for investors with a $500 portfolio, as well as those at the $1,000, $2,500, $5,000 and $10,000 levels. These are, of course, merely guidelines; your personal portfolio will vary according to your goals and investment temperament.

## THE $100 INVESTMENT PORTFOLIO

For the rock-bottom beginning investor, we recommend the following no-minimum investments:

- Money market funds or accounts (Twentieth Century Cash Reserves; see Chapter 7 for other funds)

- Stock market mutual fund (Twentieth Century Select Investors or Twentieth Century Growth)

- Automatic investment plan (Nicholas Fund or Janus Fund; minimum monthly investment, $50; see Chapter 8)

- Individual stocks purchased directly from the company (e.g., Procter & Gamble; see Chapter 8 for details)

- Closed-end stock funds (see Chapter 8 for details)

- Individual dimes and quarters (pre-1965)

At the $100 level you may wish to start out with just one of these investments and diversify as your savings grow.

## THE $500 INVESTMENT PORTFOLIO

The $500 portfolio permits a little more variety in your investments. Consider:

- Money market funds

- Stock market mutual funds (Twentieth Century funds, small brokerage account)

- Automatic investment plans (Nicholas or Janus Fund; see Chapter 8)

- VIP stock purchases (Procter & Gamble, Exxon, Texaco, and others listed in Chapter 8)

- Silver dollars, halves, quarters and dimes

To trade mutual funds, we recommend opening an account at Charles Schwab & Co. or another discount broker that caters to the small investor.

With $500, you can also begin a diversified program of investing in public companies through VIPs. For Exxon and Texaco, minimums are $250. See Chapter 8 for details.

We have purposely avoided assigning specific allocations with individual portfolios because investors have different goals and attitudes. Some investors may feel uncomfortable investing in stocks or gold and may wish to keep all of their money in a simple money market fund. Others may wish to divide their portfolios among all the categories.

## THE $1,000 INVESTMENT PORTFOLIO

The $1,000 portfolio allows you to branch out a bit further, into:

- Money market funds

- Stock market mutual funds

- Automatic investment plans

- VIP stock purchases

- Real estate

- Gold and silver coins, or gold mining funds

## THE $2,500 INVESTMENT PORTFOLIO

At the $2,500 level, you should put at least half of your money into what we consider the "basics" listed in the $100 portfolio, and choose one or two of the high-yielding but somewhat riskier areas for the rest:

- Real estate

- Foreign bank accounts

- Gold bullion coins and "junk" silver coins

- Money market funds

- Stock market mutual funds

- Automatic investment plans

- VIP stock purchases

- Numismatic coins

- Families of mutual funds (Fidelity, Vanguard, Scudder, T. Rowe Price, etc.)

- Collectibles (stamps, art, rare books, etc.)

Once you've invested in a family of mutual funds, you might want to take advantage of the telephone-switch service to maximize profits.

## THE $5,000 INVESTMENT PORTFOLIO

At the $5,000 stage, you are ready to expand further into the nontraditional markets, such as collectibles and foreign stock markets. Maintain your foundation in the basics, both for security and for liquidity. Here's a sample $5,000 portfolio:

- Money market funds

- Mutual funds (families of funds, etc.)

- Automatic investment plans

- VIP stock purchases

- Real estate

- Foreign banks

- Collectibles

- Foreign stock mutual funds

- Bullion coins, rare coins and gold and silver bullion

## THE $10,000 (OR LARGER) INVESTMENT PORTFOLIO

Only at the $10,000 level might you start thinking about speculating in commodities futures, the Eurocurrency markets, penny stocks, rare coins and some tax shelters. At this level you should consider overdraft checking accounts for emergencies and for short-term investing needs. Again, we would recommend placing half of your money in money market funds, mutual funds, VIP stock purchases and a few gold and silver coins and the remainder in other speculative ventures. The portfolio looks like this:

- Money market funds

- Mutual funds (equities, foreign markets, families of funds)

- Automatic investment plans

- VIP stock purchases

- Real estate

- Foreign currency accounts (Swiss francs, German marks, British pounds, Japanese yen, etc.)

- Collectibles

- Bullion coins, rare coins, gold bullion

- Penny stocks

- Options and futures trading

- Managed commodity accounts

- Tax shelters and limited partnerships

No need to fit all of the above investment vehicles into your portfolio. Rather, select several alternatives that suit your tastes. Spread your risks by not investing more than 25 percent in any one category. As long as inflation and economic crises threaten, gold and silver should remain a small part of your investment portfolio.

## BEST DEALS FOR THE "CASH POOR" INVESTOR

In the above investment portfolios, we have listed a variety of investment choices. Which offer the best opportunity for rapid wealth creation for the "cash poor" investor, the investor who has few liquid funds?

The "cash poor" investor can take two approaches. First is the conservative approach of putting your regular savings into long-term investments, such as growth stocks and mutual funds, to steadily increase wealth.

The second approach is to become a speculator and to make money fast. Our favorite choices for quick profits are:

1. Undervalued real estate

2. Call options on individual stocks or stock indices

3. Aggressive-growth mutual funds both here and abroad

4. Penny stocks

Remember, there is more than one way to climb the mountain of financial success. Just be careful you don't slide down the mountain by missing a toehold. Keep that conservative foundation in place with half your savings, then speculate with the rest if that is your investment temperament.

## A FINAL WORD

Your investment portfolio must grow if you are to reach financial security. Saving $100 or $1,000 is a good start, but if your investment funds remain at that level, you'll have no security. You must develop a solid savings program, as outlined in Chapter 5, to add to your investment portfolio on a consistent, monthly basis. If you follow our 10 percent savings plan and invest wisely, you will reach financial independence within a reasonable time.

You control your own financial destiny!

# CHAPTER 18

---

# Through the Valley
# of Debt

*By no means run into debt: take thine own measure,*
*who cannot live on twenty pounds a year, cannot on*
*forty.*

—Poor Richard's Almanac

WE ASKED ONE HUNDRED people what they would do if they
suddenly received $1,000. Over one-third of them replied, "Pay
off some debts." Consumer debt is one of the most serious
financial threats facing Americans today. For many people the
debt/salary ratio is so high that they must work several months
out of the year just to pay for clothing, entertainment, cars,
vacations, appliances, medical care and other goods and services
that have already been used up during previous years. It's no
wonder that most people find it so hard to get ahead. Like the
federal government, many people struggle just to keep up with
the minimum payment requirement and have no real hope of ever
paying off the balance of their debts.

And yet it was interesting to note that one-fourth of the people
we polled had no debts at all. Even more interesting was the fact
that all but one of these debt-free citizens earned less than
$15,000!

How do middle-class Americans let themselves become so over-extended? The primary cause is the easy availability of credit. Everywhere we look, consumers are bombarded with easy payment plans. In many cases "reasonable terms" has become a larger consideration for advertising purposes than the quality of the product. They make it seem almost like free money. To many people, credit has become a way of supplementing their income. They see a credit limit of, say, $500 on their billing statement and begin to think of it as money in the bank. Unfortunately, that "supplemental income" must all be repaid someday, with interest.

Among the most vulnerable targets for credit card companies are college students away from home for the first time and testing their newfound adulthood. Credit card recruiters on campus during orientation make it easy for students to open an account, often luring even the most parsimonious teens with the promise of free gifts. One family we know threw away all the credit card offers that arrived in the mail for their newly matriculated daughter, not realizing that she was receiving similar offers at her college address. Whenever the "freshman blues" hit, she went shopping—and by the end of the semester she was forced to quit school, come home and get a job to pay off her consumer debts. "Freshman blues" were nothing compared to debt reality!

Urban consumers are another target for easy-payment-plan promoters. According to a *Wall Street Journal* report, catalogs aimed at low-income urban residents highlight only the monthly payment of their purchases, not the total price. A family that couldn't afford a $449 television set will jump at the $59.64 advertised payment, never realizing that, after 19 months of payments, they will have paid $1,133.16 for a $500 TV.

Not only are consumer loans very easy to get these days, but repayment can be spread out almost indefinitely, while interest continues to mount up. Consider the following sources of easy money:

• *Major credit cards*, such as Visa and MasterCard, all offer high credit limits, with high interest rates to match. Some even exceed

18 percent. They make it very easy to get overextended by giving you 36 months or longer to pay. As long as you make the minimum monthly payment, they will continue extending you credit, and getting you deeper in debt. You don't even have to purchase something from a participating dealer—with cash advances available from most cards, you can go to the bank and receive a cash loan.

• *Department stores* must pay a percentage to the credit card company as a fee when you use a bank card such as Visa or MasterCard to make a purchase. To avoid owing this fee, most department stores and gas companies offer their own credit cards and encourage customers to use them through a myriad of tactics, including telephone solicitations, discounts for using company cards and applications prominently displayed at every cash register. Often sales personnel are instructed to invite each customer to open an account. Faced with so much easy credit, even the most stalwart debt-avoider is likely to succumb.

• *Overdraft checking accounts*, or executive lines of credit, which permit you to write checks beyond your balance, can be used for any purpose at any time. While overdraft accounts provide flexibility in personal emergencies and investment decisions, they can result in your becoming overextended because of the ease with which they are obtained. Once you qualify, you don't have to justify your reason for borrowing.

• *Installment loans* are readily available through the merchants who sell appliances, furniture, cars, etc. In many cases they will give you two or three months before you have to start making payments. By extending the day of reckoning even further into the future, this policy makes the purchase harder to resist.

With so many kinds of open-ended credit sources, it's not surprising to find that millions of Americans are over their heads in consumer debt. The rate of bankruptcy is climbing to new highs every year.

## HOW IS YOUR CREDIT RATING?

Here are some telltale signs that will indicate whether you are having trouble controlling your credit:

1. Do you owe more than 20 percent of take-home pay in consumer debts (excluding mortgages, business and auto loans)?

2. Do you pay only the minimum amount due on each bill?

3. Do you justify your credit purchases by telling yourself, "The item is on sale, so I'm saving money by buying now"?

4. Are you more than a month behind in payments for any of your debts?

5. Have you consolidated your debts to make them easier to pay?

6. Do you still owe money for items you no longer use?

7. Do you shop at certain stores because you know they will take credit cards?

8. Do you regularly write checks today, hoping to cover them with tomorrow's deposits?

9. Do you rely on your overdraft privileges, credit card cash advance, or savings account withdrawals to pay routine living expenses at the end of the month?

10. Have you considered bankruptcy the only way out?

If you answered "yes" to one or more of these questions, you could be headed for serious financial trouble. But there are steps you can take to reduce your debt exposure and gain control of your credit.

For some people, getting out of debt does indeed seem like an

impossible quest, and they simply give up. We know a couple
who seem to be the typical struggling student family. He's in
medical school, she takes care of their two small children and
they live in his sister's basement apartment. Each year they borrow $40,000 to pay for his tuition and their living expenses. You'd
think they would live frugally, knowing that in a few years he'll be
a well-paid doctor, yet every midterm break they take an expensive vacation to the Caribbean or Europe. They drive a late-model
sports car, buy brand-name clothing for the children and have
elegant wardrobes. Their reasoning? "When you're already more
than a hundred thousand dollars in debt, what's another thousand?" Newlywed couples and young people moving away from
home for the first time often make this same mistake. Faced with
the prospect of furnishing a new home or apartment, they begin
to use words like "investment" and "saving in the long run" to
justify purchasing new, top-quality items rather than shopping
for used goods or doing without for a while until they can afford
to pay cash. Thus they start out with poor financial habits right
from the beginning and continue living beyond their means
through consumer debt until they are inundated with bills they
can't pay. Investment adviser Doug Casey has said it well: "Disposable consumer goods like clothes, furniture and vacations
have little or no value to others, so it's almost always a mistake to
buy them on credit."

By contrast, consider this story, told in 1973 by a person whose
identity may surprise you.

> I was once so deeply in debt I had thought it was foolish to
> think I'd ever be out of it. I don't believe in bankruptcy, so I
> thought I was stuck for life. One day I totaled all my obligations
> and found that I owed $13,000. [This was in the mid-1960s—
> eds.] The amount seemed so enormous that I thought it was
> pointless to pay $50 or $100 against it.
>
> But I also began to feel that there wasn't anything more
> important to me than getting rid of it. I resolved to try to
> reduce it by some amount during the next couple of months. If

the effort were to make my life too miserable, I could always go back to my old spending habits; but for two months I'd concentrate on the task.

I kept a running total of my debts and reduced that total every time I made a payment against it. At the end of the first month, I'd lowered it by only $400. That meant it would take over two years to liquidate the whole amount.

But it was fun to see the total go down. Before long, no purchase was as exciting as buying a position of less debt. I was inspired to take on extra jobs—because every fee I earned meant a reduction of the total. If it became necessary to replace a household item, I did it in the cheapest possible way—knowing I could always improve upon it later. For now, cutting the debt was my most compelling motivation.

Once a momentum was created, the debt shrank faster and faster. Finally I was totally out of debt—seven months after I'd believed it would be impossible to ever get out of debt.

I happily gave up the austerity budget and went out and splurged on new clothes, dinners and dates (paying cash, of course). I never want to have to go back to such a task, so the experience kept me from ever being tempted to jump back into debt.

This story is told by Harry Browne, one of the leaders of the hard-money movement in the early 1970s and 1980s, in his book *How I Found Freedom in an Unfree World*. It's a great story because it shows how determination and setting priorities can make a seemingly impossible task not only possible, but satisfying.

We also agree with Harry's attitude toward bankruptcy. When you purchase an item and agree to pay for it, your obligation does not end simply because you've borrowed too much. "Bankruptcy" is another word for theft, even if the government says it's all right.

If you are deeply in debt, take these steps:

- List all of your obligations in a ledger where you can easily keep track of the payments and running (dwindling!) balance.

- Contact your creditors, tell them of the efforts you are making to pay off your debts and ask them to be patient.

- Pay off your smallest debts first and work up to the larger ones. It will give you great encouragement to see pages of your debt ledger crossed off completely.

- Examine your expenditures to see where you can cut back. Review Chapter 4 for help in this area.

- Take on extra jobs, and use all the extra money to pay your debts.

- Throw away your credit cards and cancel your overdraft protection. This is the only sure way to keep yourself from spending more than you earn.

- Try to avoid debt-consolidation loans that are designed to make payments easier, because they stretch out the length of your indebtedness and often increase your interest rate as well.

- Turn your assets into cash. Look through your home and sell those items that are gathering dust.

- If you have a family, make this a group effort. You will be teaching your children how important it is to honor all financial obligations, and ultimately to avoid debt.

- Be prepared to hurt if you want to change your spending patterns and get out of debt for life.

## THE RIGHT WAY TO USE CREDIT CARDS

Some people know how to use credit cards judiciously. They use them as a convenient way to purchase necessities without the risk of having to carry cash, or the nuisance of having to have checks authorized, but they always pay the entire balance every month. We like to keep a running total of our credit card purchases by recording them in a separate section of our checkbooks each time we make a purchase. That way there are no surprises at the end of the month, and we are able to avoid interest charges as well as carried-over payments. But if you use your credit card as a long-term installment loan to buy consumer goods, you're making a fundamental mistake. If you chronically borrow more than you can possibly repay, there is only one solution: Tear up all your credit cards and begin using cash or checks for all your purchases.

The only way to stop abusing your credit cards is to stop using your credit cards. This will be difficult, especially in the first month when you find yourself having to pay for both last month's credit purchases and this month's cash purchases at the same time. But it is the only sure way to keep yourself from spending more than you earn.

## DEBIT CARDS

While tearing up your credit cards is the only sure way to stop using them, there are nevertheless some occasions when you really need a card. Many stores require a major credit card for identification when you write a check. Rental agencies usually ask for a credit card number as a deposit when you rent a car, videocassette tape or other expensive item. Hotels often require either a credit card or a hefty cash deposit when you register, to cover any room service, damages or other charges you may incur. If your car breaks down or you are stranded far from home without much cash, you may find that your personal check will not be accepted by merchants or repairmen who don't know you.

You could perhaps keep a credit card tucked in your wallet "just for emergencies," but it's amazing how quickly a low checking account balance can become an emergency when a credit card is so near at hand.

Fortunately, there is an alternative to credit cards that is accepted just as readily in all these emergency situations. It is a debit card. It looks and works just like a credit card, except that instead of billing you at the end of the month, the credit card company debits your checking account immediately. The Visa cards offered by Merrill Lynch, Charles Schwab and other brokerage firms as part of their cash management accounts are also debit cards. As electronic-transfer technology improves, debit cards are becoming a regular feature of many checking accounts. They can be used at grocery stores, fast-food restaurants and any other business with the proper scanning equipment. You can "write a check" simply by zipping your card through a little machine. Just be sure to deduct the amount from your checkbook balance. Another handy feature of the debit card is that if the money isn't available in your account, the purchase will be rejected before the transaction is completed. No more hefty overdraft fees that can destroy any tight budget!

When you make a purchase with a debit card, you deduct the amount from your checkbook just as you would if you had written a check. You have the convenience of using "plastic money" without having to go into debt.

Check with banks in your area to see who offers a debit card. MasterCard II is a debit card and is part of the national Master-Card system.

If you must have a credit card, a travel-and-entertainment card such as American Express is a good compromise. It is not a debit card, but it does require you to pay off your balance every month. American Express does not extend credit beyond the monthly billing cycle except in the case of prearranged vacation-package deals. Thus you are able to arrange a short-term loan of 30 to 60 days without the temptation of extending those payments over 30 to 60 months.

## FILING BANKRUPTCY: THE HIDDEN DANGER

These tips can help you avoid future debt, but what if it is already too late for you? What if you are so deeply in debt that you see no way out? Should you file bankruptcy, as the law allows, and give yourself a fresh start?

A law passed in 1978 made it much easier to file for bankruptcy than in the past. It allows you to retain some of your property, including your home. There are many books on the market today that will tell you precisely how to go about filing for bankruptcy, including how to consolidate all of your remaining assets into the retainable home. *This isn't one of them.* Personal bankruptcy does not solve your problem; it only gives you the chance to run away from your problem temporarily. In far too many cases, the actions that led to your bankruptcy come back to haunt you. Not only do you run the risk of ruining your credit rating, but as one debt caseworker director recently warned, "Too frequently families who have filed for bankruptcy in the past year or two come to us for counseling because they soon have almost as much indebtedness as before."

Time and time again, people who have declared bankruptcy have come to us, each with the same question: "How can I regain my good credit rating?" Our question to them is, "What purpose do you have in mind?" In some cases they equate a good credit rating with a good name and reputation, which is admirable. But too often the real reason is that they crave the easy credit that got them into trouble in the first place. They seldom learn from their mistakes.

Moreover, bankruptcy is not an isolated solution to one person's problems. It can have far-reaching effects, leading to the financial downfall of others. A subscriber once wrote to us because a coin dealer had failed to deliver some coins he had ordered. We contacted the coin dealer, and discovered he was in Chapter 11 bankruptcy proceedings. We asked how he could do this to dozens of customers who had sent their money in good faith, expecting their coins to be delivered. A good businessman for over 20 years, the coin dealer was distraught but said he had no choice—two of his suppliers had recently declared bankruptcy and were now legally exempt from sending him $100,000 worth of coins for which he had already paid. He had no coins to send his customers and no money with which to send refunds. Chances are good that if we had asked those suppliers why they went bankrupt, there might have been another bankruptcy preceding theirs. And, if the coin dealer's customers had borrowed money to speculate in coins, they may have had to declare bankruptcy as well. Debt creates a precarious economy in both directions.

If you are planning to file bankruptcy, we strongly urge you to reconsider. In our opinion it is an act of irresponsibility, a fraud against the people with whom you have done business. As financial counselor Douglas R. Casey writes in his book *Strategic Investing* (Simon & Schuster, 1982), "Just because bankruptcy law is constitutional or legal doesn't mean it's ethical. Voluntary bankruptcy is theft, pure and simple. . . . Bankruptcy laws allow people to escape responsibility for their actions and, further, let them feel it's okay to do so. The laws are dehumanizing and destructive."

The only moral solution to debt is to pay off your personal loans, no matter how large they are, no matter how long it takes. We know an individual who made a serious investment error several years ago on a business venture. He had signed several loans from the bank, making him personally liable for the debt. When the business failed, he owed nearly half a million dollars. But he was a man of great personal integrity and refused to file bankruptcy. Instead, he made every effort to pay off the loan, including interest. Five years later, he had paid off almost all of his debts, at considerable personal sacrifice. You may think that this man was a fool for not taking the easy route of filing bankruptcy, yet this man has learned a vital lesson. Unlike many of us, he knows the real value of money and the risks incurred in starting a business. He is an example of what real honesty should mean in the business world, something that is all too often lacking today. More important, he is a man whom his associates trust. He will never have to worry about getting his good credit rating back, because he never lost it. His experience with debt actually increased his credibility as a businessperson.

## WHAT ABOUT CATASTROPHIC MEDICAL BILLS?

On occasion we have heard the argument that people should not be expected to pay catastrophic medical bills. Ideally, medical insurance will pay these costs, but should those who cannot afford to buy insurance or who are declared uninsurable be expected to pay the tens of thousands of dollars that a serious illness or injury might cost?

Ethically, yes. With nonelective surgery or medical care, doctors perform their labors first and send bills later. When your child has been in an accident or your spouse has a cancerous tumor, you don't want the doctor to demand payment in advance. But trust is a two-way street and today's lackadaisical attitude regarding bankruptcy could lead to just such a scenario. A doctor bill is a contractual obligation, just like any other bill, even though it is an obligation that usually comes unexpectedly during a life-or-death crisis. It may seem that you have no choice when the choice is disfigurement, disability or death. Meanwhile, bills may mount up to ten times your annual income, creating an insurmountable mountain of debt.

Nevertheless, bankruptcy should not be a first-choice solution, nor should doctors be expected to work for free. Before asking the courts to void your obligation, contact the doctor or hospital directly. Many will reduce or even forgive debts for patients who are uninsured and underpaid. Others may be more hard-nosed and will insist on full payment. That is their right. In that case, you should pay a portion toward the debt each month. As long as you are making diligent and regular payments, no matter how small, you will not be taken to court, nor will interest accrue in most cases. This is not true of banks, however, so never use credit cards or bank loans to pay medical bills.

It may take a long time, and you may never retire the loan, but you will be taking the moral and ethical road. One man we knew was involved in a traffic accident that was his fault. He had no insurance and probably could have declared bankruptcy. Many friends counseled him to do so. But he slowly paid off the debt, even while raising eight children. Twenty years later the debt was finally repaid. Meanwhile, all of his children were educated, hard-working, fine young adults who loved and admired their father. How might they have turned out if he had taught by example to run away from problems instead of accepting responsibility for one's actions?

## CONSOLIDATING YOUR LOANS

You might have the proper desire to do the right thing and pay all your creditors, but, when viewed as a whole, your entire debt burden may be truly overwhelming. Worrying about money can cause so much anxiety that some people actually commit suicide rather than face their problems. If you approach the problem systematically with a workable solution, though, you will eventually be able to eliminate your debts, and you will be able to sleep nights in the process. Let's review the steps you should take.

First, make a resolve not to add to your current debts, no matter what. Then break your debt down into manageable portions. Decide that a certain portion of your income is going to be used to pay off your debts each month. Contact your creditors and tell them of your determination to pay them in full, but admit that it may take some time. Ask them to reduce the amount you must pay each month, if necessary, or seek a consolidation loan that would allow you to combine several smaller loans into one payment. If possible, include a check for your first payment with the letter requesting an extension, to demonstrate your sincerity. Unless you have been grossly negligent in the past, they will be willing to work with you in reducing your bills. Remember, your creditors don't want to repossess your furniture or push you into bankruptcy court; they just want the money you promised to pay them.

By committing a certain portion of each paycheck to the reduction of your debt, you will give yourself a workable goal that you can live with. No longer will you face the grand total of your debts every time you sit down with your bills—you need think only about the percentage of your paycheck that will be paid this month. Having to live within your means may cause a strain on your lifestyle, but you will have such a feeling of peace as you gain control of your finances that you soon won't mind the change.

One couple who began using the evaluation techniques we describe in Chapter 3 found that they were spending nearly $100 each week in treating themselves to an elegant dinner in town. They started inviting friends over for a video and spaghetti instead, using the difference to pay off their debts. This one change reduced their annual expenditures by nearly $5,000! You can make similar changes by evaluating your habits.

Such a program may require more self-discipline than you possess, however. If you are unable to administer your own repayment schedule, you may want to seek help from a professional credit counselor. Often these services are available from various financial institutions. Consumer finance companies, commercial banks, and credit unions usually offer such consultations, sometimes at no charge. They will help you analyze your financial situation and show you ways of getting out and staying out of debt.

If you must get a consolidation loan, shop around for the best interest rate. Consumer finance companies usually charge the highest fees, as much as 24 percent. This can double your total debt in just four years! Credit unions usually charge the lowest interest on consolidation loans and provide credit counselors at no charge to members.

## PAYROLL DEDUCTION PLAN CAN HELP

If you are a member of a credit union, you may be able to take advantage of a payroll deduction plan to help pay off your loans.

Just as a payroll deduction plan is the "easy" way to save, it can also be an easy way to settle your consumer debts.

Now that interest payments on consumer loans are no longer deductible, home equity loans are becoming increasingly popular as a way to consolidate outstanding loans. Interest rates are competitive, and interest can be tax deductible. But be very careful how home equity loans are used—too many Americans are losing their homes by using them to pay off consumer debts.

## SHOULD YOU START SAVING BEFORE PAYING OFF YOUR BILLS?

Once when we were being interviewed on a radio show, we made the rather radical statement, "Savings must come first. Before the rent, before the taxes, even before food for your children, savings must be first and foremost on your list of priorities." The interviewer looked at us skeptically. "What about your debts?" he asked.

He posed an interesting question. Is it ethical to pay yourself first when you owe money to others? We have come to the conclusion that it is not only ethical; it is essential!

Savings, or the gradual accumulation of wealth, is the only road to financial security. No matter how dedicated you are to getting out of debt or to making something of yourself, you will never achieve that goal unless you are able to say, "A part of all I earn is mine to keep." Without a consistent savings program you will soon become discouraged at having to give all your money to someone else, and before long you will go back to your old spending and borrowing habits. Paying yourself first will give you the inner stability you need in order to keep paying others second, until they are completely paid off.

## BORROW MONEY TO INVEST?

While borrowing money to buy consumer products seldom makes sense, borrowing money to make sound investments sometimes does. But you must be extremely careful, because leveraging your investments can compound your losses as well as your profits.

The following are typical situations for which borrowed money may be used to make investments:

• Stocks can be bought on margin. "Margin" refers to a loan you receive from your broker, up to 50 percent of the value of the stock. This gives you leverage, as it allows you to buy up to twice as much stock for the same initial investment. If the price increases by 30 percent in a year, you make 60 percent on your investment (minus any commissions and interest charged by your broker). This is a fairly conservative leveraged position. But remember that, conversely, if the price decreases by 30 percent, you will lose 60 percent of your investment.

• Real estate is usually purchased with a mortgage. A down payment of 30 percent or less is made, and the rest of the property is financed through a mortgage or trust deed, or through several mortgages. First mortgages are usually long-term notes, lasting 15 to 30 years. Second mortgages usually have shorter maturities, lasting 5 to 10 years. Real estate is a conservative use of borrowed money as long as you make a reasonable down payment.

• Futures contracts on commodities are purchased with "good faith" deposits. The minimum deposit is usually 10 to 15 percent of the value of the contract. You will get a margin call—requiring you to pay more money or lose the contract—if the price of the commodity drops. You can lose more than your initial investment if the market goes against you.

• Starting or buying a business often involves obtaining a bank loan or financing from the previous owner or parent company.

We recommend that you be conservative at all times when using borrowed money to invest. Don't buy stocks on margin unless you know what you're doing. Futures are far more difficult to assess. Timing is extremely important; you might be right about the long-term direction of a commodity's price, but if your timing is off, you could still lose to short-term changes.

Real estate investing has had its troubles in the past decade. Play it conservatively. Don't buy into a real estate project unless your rental income will exceed your expenditures.

Above all, when borrowing money for speculating, your loans should be short term, the investment should be low risk and you should have a specific source of funds to allow you to make repayment.

## USING CREDIT IS PLAYING WITH FIRE

In sum, credit can be used to your advantage, or it can be an albatross around your neck. If you use it regularly for consumer purchases, it will become a heavy burden, but if you use it judiciously for wise and timely investments, it can be extremely profitable. Never let debt get too strong a hold on you, even for investment purposes. As Henrik Ibsen wrote in *A Doll's House*, "There can be no freedom or beauty about a home life that depends on borrowing and debt."

# CHAPTER 19

---

# What Are You Saving For?

*Money may be the husk of many things, but not the
kernel. It brings you food, but not appetite; medicine,
but not health; acquaintances, but not friends; ser-
vants, but not faithfulness; days of joy, but not peace or
happiness.*

—HENRIK IBSEN

So FAR WE HAVE discussed adjusting your spending habits, putting savings first and getting out of debt. We have given you
several investment ideas that will help your savings grow. But
what about spending your money? If you are saving for a rainy
day, do you consume your savings at the first sign of sprinkles, or
do you wait for a hurricane? What are some legitimate uses for
your long-term savings?

From time to time, emergencies arise in every household that
require large expenditures. The car or a major appliance breaks
down, a relative in a distant state dies and you need to fly to the
funeral, it's summer and you want to take a vacation. These are all
legitimate reasons for spending, but they are *not* legitimate reasons for spending your long-term savings.

For this reason, in addition to your investment funds, you
should have a *short-term savings program* to which you contribute
regularly. It should be an amount you feel comfortable with,

depending upon the extent and frequency of your financial emergencies. Perhaps 5 to 10 percent of your income would be sufficient to cover these unexpected needs. This money should be kept in an account that pays interest, but one that does not impose penalties, fees or tax ramifications for early withdrawal, which we discussed in Chapter 7. A money market fund is a good choice.

It will be easier to set this money aside if you have a specific savings goal in mind. Keep thinking, "We're saving for next summer's trip to the Grand Canyon" or "Just three more months till we can buy the new pool table." This will keep you motivated and help you avoid falling into the installment loan trap. It will also keep you from making foolish purchases. Often, by the time you have saved enough to buy something, you will discover that it was just a passing fancy. When the immediate desire wears off, you find that you really didn't want the item after all. How much better it is to realize this before it ends up collecting dust in the basement—while you are still collecting monthly bills in the mailbox!

But even with a good short-term emergency fund, you will still find legitimate uses for your long-term investments at various stages in your life.

## BUYING A HOME

One of the most important purchases you will ever make is your own home. Much more than physical shelter, it can provide an inner security and community stability that are available through few other sources. Herbert Hoover extolled the virtues of home ownership by saying:

> A family that owns its home takes pride in it, maintains it better, gets more pleasure out of it, and has a more wholesome, healthful and happy atmosphere in which to bring up children.
> The homeowner has a constructive aim in life. He works

harder outside his home; he spends his leisure more profitably; and he and his family live a finer life and enjoy more of the comforts and cultivating influences of our modern civilization.

A husband and wife who own their own home are more apt to save. They have an interest in the advancement of a social system that permits the individual to store up the fruits of his labor. As direct taxpayers, they take a more active part in local government.

Above all, the love of home is one of the finest instincts and the greatest of inspirations of our people.

Studies have shown that homeowners tend to vote and participate in local community affairs more than apartment dwellers. They do not move as often as renters. They are even less likely to get a divorce. And they tend to have fewer financial problems, even though they have greater debt because of the mortgage on the house. In short, homeowners tend to be more responsible individuals. As *The Wall Street Journal* stated recently, "Homeowners are more likely to vote, less likely to move, and have a greater incentive to keep up the appearance of the neighborhood." This is not to say that all renters are irresponsible, of course, but on the average, homeowners tend to be more responsible and involved in the community than renters.

Buying your own home should be the first goal of every saver. Use your long-term savings program as a means to achieve home ownership. You should not use all your savings for this single investment, but you should actively work toward owning a home as an important element of your investment portfolio.

## Use a Conservative Approach

You may want to be a speculator and take calculated risks in other markets, but we recommend a conservative approach when it comes to buying your own home. Put as much money down as you can, and don't take out a second mortgage unless it's absolutely essential. Even though there are tax advantages to keeping a mortgage indefinitely, plan on paying off your home someday. There are even more advantages to owning your home free and clear. You'll sleep better knowing that, in this uncertain economy, your home is not at risk.

## EDUCATION

There are other worthwhile uses for your investment savings as well. Education is one of these. It can legitimately be called an investment in yourself, because money spent now will pay off with future dividends in the form of a better job, higher pay, greater knowledge and increased enjoyment of life. While you shouldn't spend all your savings on any single category, a good portion of your investment funds could be earmarked for college.

But parents should not feel that they owe their children a college education at the top university in the nation. It is nice to help them if you can afford it, but it is sad to see how many people borrow money to put their children through school, often by taking out hefty second mortgages on their homes. By the time the last child is educated and launched toward a high-paying career, the parents are left with nothing but bills and a bewildered feeling of "Is this all we have achieved after thirty years of work?"

Students who make sacrifices for their education generally perform better than those who receive tuition checks without any more personal effort than it takes to write home for more money. They study harder, choose their classes more carefully, set career goals earlier and graduate sooner. Even if it means starting at a local junior college and then moving on to a better-known university, these students come out ahead.

Still, few young people earn enough money to pay the exorbitant tuition and fees charged at the top universities across the country. Therefore, it is important that you make saving for college a family project. Let your children know about your 10 percent savings program. Help them understand the choices and sacrifices involved in sticking with it. They may not be able to earn all they need for college themselves, but they will have the benefit of knowing that some of your savings came from their willingness to forgo a new bike, expensive clothes and other luxuries that would have reduced the family savings.

In addition, teach your children from a young age to appreciate the value of both work and thrift. Encourage them to study well and make education a top priority. Help them see that a scholarship is ultimately more valuable than the money that can be saved from an after-school job paying minimum wages, particularly if that job causes your students' grades to drop.

## Investing in Zero-Coupon Bonds

One way to save for college is to invest in *zero-coupon bonds*.

Zero-coupon bonds are a relatively recent innovation in the bond market. Ordinary bonds come with a set of coupons to last the life of the bond, and the investor simply clips the coupons at regular intervals and cashes them in at a bank or other financial institution. Zeros come without coupons because no interest is paid until the bond matures. This allows the company to defer both the principal and interest on its debt. Interest continues to accrue at compounded rates. Except for municipal zeros (which are always tax exempt), the interest is taxable in the year it accrues, even though it hasn't been collected yet. In essence, this becomes a forced savings plan, since you must pay the tax out of other income and leave the zero-coupon bond intact.

The big advantage to zeros is that you are forced to reinvest all earnings. Consequently, you can see dramatic increases in your capital when you redeem the bond. Moreover, since there is a secondary market in zeros, you can regain your cash at any time (although you may not get the price you expected, since zeros are highly volatile).

We see three main uses for zero-coupon bonds. First, they are excellent for education expenses. You could buy a $5,000 bond in your new baby's name and have $35,000 available when the child is ready for college. To protect yourself from inflation and higher interest rates, buy a series of short-term bonds over the years, thus keeping up with fluctuating rates.

An advantage to zeros is that they can be purchased at extremely low minimums, some for less than $200, so they are ideal for starting a child investing toward his own future.

Another good use for zeros is in your retirement fund. Again, buy only medium-term bonds of no more than eight years, and stagger their purchase so you have one maturing every year or two. Then roll them over into new bonds at prevailing rates, or put the money into another investment that may have come along in the meantime, until you are ready to use the cash for income.

Financing a home can also be made easier with zeros. Suppose you need an additional $10,000 between the down payment and the first mortgage, but you have only $3,000 in hand. Your monthly income is already stretched to the hilt, and you can't afford more than an interest-only loan on the $10,000. You could buy a $3,000 zero, make your interest-only payments, and in 10 years your bond will have earned enough to pay off the balance. Or, instead of taking out a second mortgage, you could offer to use that same money to buy a zero for the seller, perhaps showing him how it will be worth $21,000 in just 20 years, more than twice what you owe him!

Zeros can be purchased from any major brokerage firm, including discount brokers like Charles Schwab. Kidder Peabody (10 Hanover Square, 14th Floor, New York, NY 10005, 800-345-8502 or 212-510-5401) is another reliable company that specializes in zero-coupon bonds.

One final comment on education. If you are a medical, law or dental student who has incurred heavy debts to pay for your education, be especially careful when you finally start earning money. According to one psychologist, professionals are the "worst investors" because they spend so many years in training that they have a "pent-up hunger" to make money fast. If you are in this situation, be circumspect when it comes to investing your hard-earned savings. Doctors and dentists are notorious for making bad investment decisions or getting involved in get-rich-quick schemes! And be sure to save 10 percent of your income even while you are paying off your student debts.

## STARTING A FAMILY

Most financial counselors today recommend that couples wait until they are financially set before starting a family or adding another child, and that they limit the number of children to just one or two. They cite studies proclaiming the cost of raising a child to be $180,000 or more as reason for this advice. However, while there is no denying that raising a family is more expensive than living alone, some decisions should be based on more than financial impact alone, and this is one of them.

In the first place, those studies are often misleading, assuming that everything you provide for your child will be purchased brand-new, at department-store prices. But, as we demonstrated in Chapter 4, there are dozens of ways to readjust your personal cost of living. Thousands of couples—and single parents as well—manage to raise families with far less money than these studies have determined is necessary. It *can* cost $180,000 to raise a child, but it doesn't have to.

Secondly, and perhaps more important, there is no greater joy than that which comes from raising children. Yes, there are sacrifices to be made when young parents are still finishing college or starting new careers, and financial security makes the transition easier. But emotional stability is more important than financial security when determining the size and timing of family additions. If you truly want a family, your budget will adjust.

### How Much Does It Cost To Work?

Perhaps your children have already arrived, and you are facing the challenges of being a two-income family. Should you both work away from home? And do you have a choice?

A recent edition of the comic strip "For Better or for Worse" shows a young mother exulting over having enrolled her toddler in an all-day day-care center that has a long waiting list. "I can't believe the freedom!" she exclaims to a friend. Then she adds, less enthusiastically, "I can't believe the expense."

Throughout the past two decades it has become increasingly expected that women will work outside the home. Many have put off childbearing while they attend college and then establish careers. When babies do enter the picture, it seems like a natural thing to take three months off and then return to work with the child safely in the care of someone else. For women in high-paying professional positions, the decision to continue working can be financially sound: She can afford to hire someone else to perform domestic duties, and spend her leisure time with her family. Often the job she has chosen is rewarding and fulfilling rather than tiring and stressful. But the average working mother is often limited to lower-paying jobs. She doesn't want to leave her children with someone else, but she feels that the family budget needs her added income.

It is to this woman that we address this section. If you have gone back to work chiefly to supplement your husband's income, consider these costs of working:

• *Child care.* This will vary according to where you live, how many hours you are away and what kind of care your desire. You might find a neighbor willing to do it for $10 a day, or you might hire a live-in nurse at $200 a week plus room and board. Most likely your child-care costs will be somewhere in between. It is a fixed cost, one you can budget for each month.

However, many costs of working are less straightforward:

• *Transportation.* It's easy to figure how much you spend on gas and oil, but what about wear and tear? You may need to buy a new car sooner than expected, which could add thousands to your actual cost of working.

• *Clothing.* If you choose an occupation that requires a uniform, you're in luck. You can get by with two or three work outfits. But most working women find it necessary to purchase a half dozen outfits every season for wearing to the office. Moreover, working mothers spend more money on their children's clothing than do home mothers, because they don't have time to shop for sales or to sew. In fact, shopping is often put off until the need is greatest—and the prices are highest. For the working woman, time is money.

• *Food.* When you're at home, lunch costs practically nothing. Just fix a sandwich or warm up some leftovers that might otherwise be thrown out. When you're away from home, though, the cost of lunch can mount up. Some employers provide kitchen facilities, but for many, lunch becomes a small cost that adds up fast.

Evening meals become more expensive as well. It's so much easier to stop off for carry-out food on the way home, or to pick up expensive prepared entrées from the frozen food section, or to go out to a favorite restaurant than to face the kitchen stove at night. For many families, food costs double when Mom is working. Ours did.

• *Domestic costs.* Some working women hire a maid, some spend all day Saturday cleaning, and some just learn to live with the clutter and dust. However you choose to deal with it, cleaning and other household chores are a greater burden for working women. Usually the solutions cost money. In fact, my housekeeper earns more than my friend earns as a substitute teacher.

• *Taxes.* When combined with your husband's income, your job could push you into a higher tax bracket, sending most of your marginal income (that's *your* paycheck) to the IRS.

• *Higher standard of living.* Many women go to work to increase family income for consumption purchases. Often couples will make expensive installment purchases on the strength of the wife's new earnings. The result is that they are deeper in debt and have less disposable income than before she started working. If you are a woman who considers her job a temporary stage—to help pay off some debts, for example, or as a career to enjoy before children enter the picture—don't get used to spending that income. Save your entire paycheck, or use it to pay off old debts. Then you will be able to quit when you feel that your family needs you at home.

• *Emotional costs.* No matter how wonderful your partner may be, it is the woman who bears the brunt of the dual jobs. Trying to work, maintain a household, provide loving guidance to children and retain a position as the soul of the home causes many women to suffer both psychologically and physically. What remains of your paycheck could end up in your doctor's wallet.

We're not saying that all women should stay at home; far from it. Many women gain a great deal of satisfaction and fulfillment from their jobs, especially if they don't have small children to worry about. Other women, divorced or widowed, have no choice but to work. But there are a growing number of mothers who feel pushed into the workplace, to supplement the family income. To them we say: Add up the costs, *all* the costs, and then make your decision. You may be working for peanuts.

## STARTING A NEW BUSINESS

It has been said that you'll never get rich working for someone else. As we suggested in Chapter 15, you may want to start your own business, either as a part-time supplement to your present job or as a full-time venture.

You may want to take over an already existing business, buy a new franchise of a national chain or become a salesperson in one of the dozens of multilevel sales organizations around today. If you are more adventurous, you may want to start something completely new. Perhaps you have a particular skill, such as photography or carpentry, that is in high demand. You may want to manufacture and market a product you have designed. Owning your own business can bring an immense sense of satisfaction, as well as the opportunity of earning a lot of money.

This is not something you should jump into, however. You

need to study the product and test the market to make sure there is sufficient demand for the goods or services you plan to sell. If you are buying a business from someone else, find out why he wants to sell. Are you buying liabilities as well as assets? Look at the records for the previous three years. Have profits declined, increased or fluctuated wildly? If it is a franchise business, what would your relationship be to the parent company? How much freedom will you have in making marketing decisions?

Starting a brand-new business is risky, but it can lead to the greatest personal rewards. Be flexible, and keep it simple at first. We know of several would-be entrepreneurs who began their businesses by renting expensive office space and hiring secretaries and assistants before any money started coming in. Because of the heavy overhead expenses, the businesses never had a chance. On the other hand, a woman we know sold homemade lunches once a week to workers near her home. She started with just three customers, doing all the work herself in her own kitchen. Within a year she was providing 150 lunches a day with a part-time staff of four other homemakers.

When starting a new business, it is important to remember the value of diversification. Don't put all of your investment money into one venture. Do all you can to make a business work, but also be realistic. Don't stubbornly hang on if it becomes apparent that you've made a mistake. Be willing to cut your losses, if necessary, and try something else.

## CHARITY

Midas, the legendary miser, learned too late that accumulating gold is not the sure road to happiness. His lust for wealth cost him his friends, his health, his daughter and his happiness. Amassing a fortune to count and to gloat over should not be the primary goal of your savings program; your savings should be used as a tool for bringing long-term happiness to yourself and to others.

One of the ways to do this is to give some of your money to

worthwhile charities and other organizations. At one time the wealthy felt it was their duty to share a portion of their estates with those less fortunate than they. All the great charitable foundations were created by wealthy individuals who wanted to help others, but as the federal government has created more and more welfare programs, the charitable instinct in America has dwindled. Americans have begun to rely too heavily on the government as a fairy godmother to solve the problem of poverty. But government programs have not been successful. Private charities still serve a vital need in this country, and they deserve your support.

There are thousands of private charities, emphasizing hundreds of different projects, from medical research and education to environmental concerns and refugee relief. Churches, political candidates, schools and community service organizations all seek financial contributions. Most organizations are run by dedicated, hard-working people, many of them volunteers, who make sure that the largest portion of contributions is spent on the project for which it was intended. But be sure to investigate the goals and past performance of any organization before you contribute. Some charitable foundations have such heavy overhead expenses that 80 to 90 percent of the funds they collect are spent on employee salaries and other operating expenses. Be especially wary of organizations with flashy fund-raising campaigns.

In addition to full-scale organizations, charity can often begin closer to home. We have gained a great deal of personal satisfaction from contributing money to our church and local college, helping to pay for the education and religious missions of young people we know, and giving low-cost loans to young couples needing down payment money for their first homes. With just a few hundred dollars, you may be able to make a lasting difference in the life of someone you know.

As financial counselors, we have learned of numerous individuals who eventually died and left behind very large estates. In many cases, they slaved away at making a living without enjoying life to the fullest. They lived parsimonious lives, planning on leaving hundreds of thousands of dollars to their children. But more often than not, inherited money does more harm than good to your children. It gives them the attitude of getting "something for nothing," and they often spend it frivolously. We believe that after providing for the essential needs of your dependents, it is a much wiser course to transfer your estate to a worthy cause, whether it be political, religious, educational, scientific or charitable in nature. If you don't see a good school, church or other organization worthy of your contributions, consider establishing your own trust or nonprofit organization to achieve your objectives.

## Tax Benefits of Giving to Charity

Your main reason for contributing to charity will be your desire to support a specific cause, but there are financial benefits as well. Contributions made to nonprofit organizations are tax deductible. You can reduce your tax burden even further by contributing appreciated assets rather than cash. Suppose, for example, that you bought 100 shares of a company when their price was $50 a share. If you sold the stock at $100, you would have to pay capital gains taxes on $5,000, the amount by which they had appreciated. But if you donate the shares to charity, you will receive a tax deduction for the full $10,000 and not owe any tax on the gain.

You can also set up a *charitable remainder trust* with your favorite charity, college, public foundation or other nonprofit organization. Using a charitable remainder trust, you can give away a substantial amount of money, receive a tax deduction and still receive an annuity for life from the public charity. You can donate stocks, a piece of property or other asset for which you can take a tax deduction. In return, you will start receiving a lifetime annuity. When you die, the charitable organization will own the property or asset that you donated.

## PERSONAL CATASTROPHES

Sometime during your life you may face a personal crisis. You may lose your job, experience a long-term illness or suffer the death of your spouse. If this should happen, it will be a great relief to you to know that you have a large investment portfolio to draw on until you can get back to work. You will probably have to cut back somewhere on your lifestyle, but the experience will not leave you destitute. You will not risk losing your home, car and other necessities.

Even though you will be using your savings during this time, you should continue to save 10 percent of whatever income you receive, whether it be from disability or unemployment insurance, assistance from relatives, Social Security, or pension payments. It may seem pointless to save money and withdraw it at the same time, but there are two important reasons for continuing to do this. First, you don't want to break the habit of saving. Once the crisis has passed, it will be too easy to keep saying, "Next month we'll start saving again." Second, this system will ensure that you never run completely out of money. Your savings may dwindle precariously, but you will always have at least 10 percent of what you received from your last check.

It is important that you recognize the difference between a true emergency and a simple setback. The problem should be severe enough to cut your current income by more than half, and it should be expected to last more than a month or two to qualify as a true crisis. Investigate other sources before you begin using your long-term savings to cover routine living expenses. If you do use your savings, decide ahead of time at what point you will be able to stop, and then stick with that decision. The very fact that you need to use it should convince you of the importance of maintaining your investment program.

## RETIREMENT

The golden years are what you have been saving for. Now, if you could just be sure of how many golden years you will have, it would be easier to know how much you can spend!

Even though you may no longer be earning a salary after you retire, this does not mean that you will not be receiving income.

In fact, you probably will have several sources of revenue each month, perhaps including Social Security benefits, a corporate pension, military retirement pay, investment dividends, rental income and annuities. You may find that these sources of income are sufficient for your daily needs, but if you need to supplement your regular retirement income, there is a way to use your long-term savings sensibly without having to worry about running out of funds.

First, continue to pay yourself 10 percent. This is a lifelong habit, not something you should practice only during your earning years. Your income, and consequently the amount you save, may be smaller now, but it is essential that you continue saving and investing so that you don't run out of money during your lifetime.

There are several ways that you can use your savings without endangering the principal. One possibility is to have dividends sent to you directly in a monthly or quarterly check instead of reinvesting the dividends as you did during your earning years. During the building years you want to invest as much as possible, so it makes sense to reinvest your dividends, but now that you need income to live on, you can spend your dividends without touching your principal.

Systematically selling your gold and silver coins is another way to supplement retirement income. You will still want to keep some coins on hand as a hedge against political uncertainty and economic crisis, but if you have been stockpiling them over the years (through a coin-of-the-month plan, for example), you can afford to sell a few without jeopardizing your personal security.

Rental income can be another source for paying daily expenses. Most people use their rental income to make their mortgage payments, but if you have paid the mortgage off in full, you can use the income from your rental properties for your living expenses. Another way to gain retirement income from your investment real estate would be to sell it and take back a first or second mortgage, thus providing monthly income without having to be a landlord anymore.

## Don't Die Rich, Live Rich!

Finally, if you are still a good many years away from retirement, remember that there is more to enjoying life than having plenty of money. In our own travels, we have had the opportunity of sharing many tours with retired people. Some are wonderfully fit and enjoy every minute of their travels. But others are sadly in very poor health.

*Good health* cannot be purchased with money, and yet it is free to those who are willing to put forth the effort. With the cost of health care rising at a phenomenal rate, you simply can't afford not to eat well, exercise regularly and take good care of your body. Proper dental care is equally important, and the cost of semiannual checkups is nominal compared to the price of cavities, caps, gum disease and dentures.

Equally important, but often overlooked in this hurry-up world, is the need for *adequate rest*. You may not need the average eight hours of sleep each night—some people need ten hours, others are rejuvenated with just six—but if you don't rest enough for your personal needs, you could end up with chronic fatigue, high susceptibility to infection, depression and even a nervous breakdown. All are costly.

Another often-neglected aspect of good health is adequate *socializing*. Employers learned long ago that coffee breaks and office chatting actually increase worker productivity, but too many career-oriented people, and particularly working wives and mothers, never find time for friendship. Make time.

Health care is expensive, but there are ways to reduce the costs. Medical insurance and participation in health maintenance organizations (HMOs) are obvious ways to limit costs. Many counties provide free services for immunizations and testing for glaucoma, blood pressure and various diseases. Medical and dental schools provide supervised care at greatly reduced rates by students who will be charging normal fees in just a year or two.

*Spiritual development* is essential as well. There has to be more to life than just accumulation of wealth and material goods. Your own formula for spiritual development will be very personal, and we wouldn't presume to give specifics. You might rely on an organized religion, or you may prefer a more individualized philosophy.

You should search for a philosophy that brings inner peace first of all. It should result in a more caring attitude toward your spouse and children, and a genuine concern for others that will lead to good deeds and actions. It should also make you a more humble and forgiving person, one who doesn't insist on being "me first" and having your own way. Ultimately, it should prepare you to face hardship and suffering with courage and serenity. If you have developed these qualities, you will be happy, even in the face of adversity.

Decide today that you will exercise regularly, eat properly, quit smoking and not worry about things you can't change. Moreover, remember that a long life can be a burden to the lonely. Don't be so busy earning money that you neglect the loved ones in your life. Your family's personal needs should always come before material needs. Also, learn to develop character traits that will make you the kind of person others like to be around. The person who has friends and the respect of associates is wealthy indeed.

If you keep these personal and financial goals in mind, they will pay lifelong dividends that can be reinvested again and again.

# CHAPTER 20

---

# Who Will Inherit
# Your Money?

*A long life may not be good enough but a good life is
long enough.*

—Poor Richard's Almanac

As we near the end of this book, one pressing question remains: How will you pass your hard-earned estate on to your loved ones with the least possible tax liabilities? In other words, who will inherit your investment portfolio—your children, your favorite charity or the government? No matter how many thousands of dollars you may earn by using the techniques outlined in this book, financial success won't be yours until you have arranged for your chosen beneficiaries to gain control of your estate.

Thousands of Americans die every year without even writing a will, let alone preparing to avoid estate taxes. Consequently, the important decisions of how the property of an estate is to be divided are made by state laws rather than by the desires of the deceased. And the court will follow the cold, unemotional guidelines established by the state.

If your estate is worth more than $600,000 (not unlikely, these days), the consequences of procrastination are greater. Federal inheritance taxes can take as much as 55 percent of your estate, depending on its size. Many states also impose their own inheritance taxes. It is not unusual for heirs to walk away from probate proceedings with only half of an estate intact—victims of the court, probate lawyers and tax collectors. This is especially crushing to a spouse who has shared equally in the building of an estate but now faces both widowhood and reduced assets simply because her husband died. All of this can be avoided with relatively little effort or expense through proper estate planning.

The wealthy have had the financial means and legal know-how to preserve multimillion-dollar estates for generations. They have used highly paid attorneys to help them avoid inheritance taxes through nonprofit, tax-free foundations and educational and charitable organizations. Most of us can't afford such expensive services, but we can take advantage of some loopholes used by the wealthy to avoid probate costs and estate taxes. This chapter will present several simple but effective ways to keep your assets outside your estate, so that when you die your heirs will not lose your money when they lose your companionship.

## HAVE A FINANCIAL "CHECKUP" ANNUALLY

Just as you should have a medical exam regularly, so should you have a financial checkup periodically to correct past mistakes and to spot new ones. This checkup should begin by determining exactly how large your estate is.

Greedy government, nosy neighbors and cutthroat competitors all pose significant threats to your personal and professional privacy and provide legitimate reasons for taking steps to keep your life from reading like an open book. Privacy is indeed an important issue. But when a death occurs, too much privacy can be worse than no privacy at all. Huge bank accounts established in distant cities, often under assumed names, eventually are absorbed by the institution because no heirs know about the money; millions of dollars are lost because no claims are ever filed against unknown life insurance policies; widows and heirs squander lifetime estates because they have no experience with handling money.

These problems can be avoided by taking a few simple precautions. You can still maintain a large degree of your financial privacy while ensuring that your money is not so well hidden that it may become lost forever.

The first thing to do is find someone you can trust. If you are married, the logical person would be your spouse. If you are single, you might confide in a parent, brother or sister, adult child or attorney. Your purpose is to make sure this person knows enough about your affairs to handle your estate if you become disabled or die.

Here are some basic items you should discuss and record:

• *Income tax returns.* A good place to begin is with your tax return. It is compact, organized and presents a fairly accurate and comprehensive picture of your annual income.

• *Insurance policies.* It may seem obvious, yet hundreds of thousands of dollars in benefits go unpaid each year simply because no one ever files a claim. You might be covered by policies your spouse doesn't know about, particularly if this is a second marriage. Write down the company, agent's name, beneficiaries, type of policy, amount of coverage and method of filing a claim for all your death benefits, including military benefits, pension funds, teachers' annuities and employer policies. Make sure the benefits are assigned to the right person—more than one second wife has been dismayed to discover that the first wife is still the beneficiary, simply because the husband never got around to making the change. If you have minor children from a previous marriage, you may want to purchase a separate policy to protect them.

• *Bank accounts.* As financial affairs become more complicated, you may find yourself with half a dozen separate bank accounts. You may have a legitimate reason for wanting to keep a secret bank account, but be sure to leave a record of the bank address, account number and any other pertinent instructions so someone can find and claim the money when you die.

• *Safe-deposit boxes.* Like bank accounts, these often remain unclaimed. Keep a list of all private vaults, safe-deposit boxes, combinations and locations of personal safes and treasure maps—yes, people still hide coins in their backyards!

• *Individual investments.* Just adding two or three new investments to your portfolio each year can amount to dozens of individual stocks, tax shelters, properties or accounts over a lifetime. It can be extremely helpful to review these investments periodically, perhaps once a year when you are preparing your tax return, to determine whether you should continue to hold them. If you are married and your spouse has always handled the investments, it is even more critical that you begin discussing that person's choices and sharing in the decision-making process, so you will be prepared to continue the estate if your spouse should die before you. If you are unmarried but rely on an attorney or investment adviser to manage your money, insist that your portfolio be explained to you. Then take an active role in your investments.

• *Real estate.* You should have a separate folder for every property you own to facilitate assessing the profitability of each. The folder should contain documents from the purchase of the house, receipts for repairs, payment stubs, rental income record, depreciation schedule and appraisal updates. You should also jot down why you selected that particular property. Sometimes future plans for a property die with the owner, and an opportunity for profit may be lost.

• *Debts.* Keep a list of your outstanding bills and compare them to your income. If you are spending more than 20 percent of your take-home pay on consumer debts (excluding mortgage, education and possibly auto loans), you should examine your spending habits and reevaluate your priorities.

• *Current will.* Everyone needs one, but no one likes to think about it. If you don't have a written will, the courts will use a generic will determined by your state's laws. Look at the inheritance laws for your state and decide whether you want your estate distributed in that way. It may be just the incentive you need to finally get to the attorney and write your own will.

• *Previous commitments.* If you are contemplating marriage, you need to discuss previous commitments that you and your fiancé may already have made to help in the support of children, elderly parents or charitable organizations.

## WHY ESTATE PLANNING?

Even if you are a young investor and relatively unconcerned about the size of your estate at this point, you should consider the reasons for estate-planning techniques. All too frequently, investors wait until their estate becomes so large that it would be extremely difficult to avoid inheritance taxes. Advance planning and continued updating are the key.

Changes in estate tax law do not mean you need no longer plan carefully. Inflation will continue to increase the value of your estate. Taxes will be due on the surviving spouse's estate within nine months of your passing! Thus, few people are exempt from the need for estate planning.

## WHERE THERE'S A WILL, THERE'S A LAWYER

Once you know how much you have, it is time to determine how your estate should be distributed if you should die. You need to draw up a legally binding will.

Everyone should have a will. But even with a will, if your estate is the least bit complicated—several heirs, large holdings or non-family beneficiaries such as charitable organizations—your estate could be tied up for more than a year before your heirs receive anything. Moreover, legal fees can amount to as much as one-fourth of your estate!

What causes these expensive delays? Probate.

What exactly is probate?

The term *probate* comes from the root word *prove*, which means "test." Probating a will, then, means testing its validity. If you are the sole owner of a property, when you die it is as though your name is deleted from the title and the asset no longer has a legal owner. A court order is required to transfer ownership, and the judge must decide who that new owner will be. If the deceased left a will, then the judge's job is much easier. He is bound to follow the deceased's instructions as far as possible. But he will first have to ascertain that this is indeed the most recent will, legally worded and signed by the deceased (not forged by someone else). Its requirements will also be tested to see if they comply with state laws.

It would seem easy to verify the validity and legality of a will's requirements, but because of backlogs and other delays, it takes 16 months for an average estate to go through probate. If there are unhappy heirs, partners or creditors who are contesting the will, probate can take much longer and cost much more.

One of the first steps, particularly if you have a simple estate of less than $600,000 and a single heir (your spouse), is to take advantage of joint ownership. Any asset you own individually will be probated, even if you have a will and a surviving spouse as the sole beneficiary. Consequently, unless you have other reasons for single ownership such as children from a previous marriage, protecting assets from possible lawsuits or anticipating divorce, you and your spouse should have joint ownership of all your assets.

For more complicated estates, there is another method of avoiding probate. Once used only by the rich, it has gained popularity among average Americans over the past several years. The method? Setting up a trust.

## ESTABLISHING A LIVING TRUST

Because the trust itself does not die, its ownership of the properties does not have to be probated. At the time of the owner's death, the executors of the estate simply follow the instructions given to the trust, distributing the assets in the way the deceased wanted them to be distributed. There are still some legal fees, of course, but no lengthy and exorbitant probate proceedings.

The majority of estates are simple enough that a trust can be set up by the individual without costly attorney's fees. You will still need a lawyer to write your will, but with sufficient information you can actually prepare your estate for distribution yourself. Other estates may be more complicated, and you will want to consult a trust attorney.

Probably the easiest trust to set up is the *simple beneficiary trust,* called the *living trust* because it can be changed while you are still living and then lives on after you die.

With a simple beneficiary trust, you are your own trustee, continuing to manage your assets as you always have. You can change the stipulations in the will at any time. Obviously, since you are the administrator, there are no administrative fees. One important consideration is assigning a successor for yourself—a person to administer the distribution of the trust after you die. Once your trust is established, you will need to transfer all of your assets to the trust's name. Thereafter, whenever you make an investment or purchase a valuable item, it should be listed under the trust's name.

If you are interested in writing your own trust, there is an outstanding book called *It's Easy To Avoid Probate,* by Barbara J. Stock (Linch Publishing, Box 75, Orlando, FL 32802, 800-327-7055), that will tell you exactly how to do it. It even includes sample trusts, so you can copy the format and fill in your specific details. The author recommends that you have an attorney check your work, however, to make certain it has been worded correctly and legally.

## HOW TO KEEP ASSETS OUT OF YOUR ESTATE

One of the best ways to avoid estate taxes is to systematically reduce the size of your estate. It takes careful planning, so it is vital that you begin now.

The best approach is to create several irrevocable trusts. For example, you may wish to set up your own tax-free charitable foundation, which can be engaged in educational, scientific or religious pursuits. Once you have established this tax-free foundation, assets in the foundation are no longer part of your estate. It is a method commonly used by the wealthy to avoid estate taxes.

Another alternative is a charitable trust, whereby you donate assets to your favorite charity, thus removing the property from your estate. You can have the organization pay you a lifetime annuity in exchange for the donation. The rules can be complex, but many charitable organizations will be more than willing to explain to you how it works.

In addition, you can transfer assets to your children before your death and thus avoid inheritance taxes. Each year you and your spouse can give up to $10,000 to each of your children (or to anyone else for that matter) without owing a gift tax. We actually don't recommend this because we feel that "free money" can do more harm than good to your children, but it is a system used by thousands each year.

Another way to transfer assets is to have your heirs purchase your home or other expensive items, either as a straight sale or as an annuity. The "new owners" make a mortgage or annuity payment to you, and you pay them rent. When you die, the house already belongs to your heirs and thus avoids probate.

## DISINHERIT THE IRS THROUGH LIFE INSURANCE

Life insurance is an excellent way for anyone to provide the liquid funds necessary to pay off Uncle Sam and allow your estate to be passed along intact to your heirs. Life insurance provides instant money when your family and heirs need it the most.

Second-to-die insurance policies are especially useful as an estate-planning tool. Under current federal estate laws, you can avoid estate taxes initially by turning over your entire estate to your surviving spouse. However, when your spouse passes on, your estate will then be subject to confiscatory estate taxes. To keep your estate within your family, a second-to-die policy works perfectly. It's considerably cheaper than a straight individual life insurance policy.

If you want more information about second-to-die insurance policies and which companies offer the best rates, obtain a free copy of "Disinherit the IRS," by David T. Phillips, independent insurance agent, David T. Phillips & Co., 3200 N. Dobson Rd., Building C, Chandler, AZ 85224, 800-223-9610. There is no obligation and no salesperson will call.

# Seven Golden Rules for Financial Success

> *To be a philosopher is not merely to have subtle thoughts, nor even to found a school, but so to love wisdom as to live accordingly to its dictates, a life of simplicity, independence, magnanimity, and trust.*
>
> —HENRY DAVID THOREAU

IN THE PRECEDING PAGES we have given you many principles and rules that will help you become financially successful. The following seven rules are a summary of this book:

1. Put savings first.
2. Save at least 10 percent of your income.
3. Make it easy to deposit your savings.
4. Make it difficult to withdraw your savings.
5. Invest your savings wisely.
6. Control your spending.
7. Control your debt.

By following these simple rules, you can become financially secure and still have the freedom to spend your money and enjoy your life.

# Index

# About the Authors

MARK SKOUSEN is editor of *Forecasts & Strategies,* one of the largest investment newsletters in the United States. He is Adjunct Professor of Economics and Finance at Rollins College in Winter Park, Florida and the author of 14 books. He received his Ph.D. in economics from George Washington University, and he is a former economist with the Central Intelligence Agency.

JO ANN SKOUSEN is assistant editor of *Forecasts & Strategies* and the former editor of *Money Letter for Women.* She has coauthored several books with her husband. She has organized and participated in a variety of investment conferences and seminars around the world.

The Skousens are the parents of five children and reside in Winter Park, Florida.